Cross-Cultural Explorations

It is only in recent decades that psychology as an academic discipline has begun to recognize the importance of a cultural perspective. From cross-cultural psychology through to psychological anthropology, psychologists have taken a number of approaches to studying the role of culture in human behavior.

This comprehensive workbook is designed to facilitate students' understanding and application of major concepts and principles of culture and psychology. The fully updated new edition features over 100 case studies, self-administered scales, mini-experiments, and library research projects, addressing topics such as culture, race/ethnicity, gender, age, sexual orientation, disability, and social class. Theoretical and guiding content is included in each chapter to embed the activities within key concepts and principles. In addition, the workbook is supported by a substantial Instructor's Manual that includes discussion questions, video recommendations, variations by course level, and suggestions for expanded writing assignments.

Designed to contribute to the inclusion of cultural perspectives in the psychology curriculum, this wide-ranging book provides students with hands-on experiences that facilitate the understanding and application of major concepts and principles in the study of culture and psychology.

Susan B. Goldstein received her PhD in Psychology from the University of Hawaii while a grantee of the East West Center. She is a Professor of Psychology at the University of Redlands where she teaches cross-cultural psychology as well as study abroad pre-departure and re-entry courses. Her research and publications have focused on study abroad, intercultural attitudes, social justice allies, stigma, and strategies for diversifying the psychology curriculum.

Cross-Cultural Explorations

Activities in Culture and Psychology

Third Edition

Susan B. Goldstein

Routledge
Taylor & Francis Group

NEW YORK AND LONDON

Third edition published 2019
by Routledge
52 Vanderbilt Avenue, New York, NY 10017

and by Routledge
2 Park Square, Milton Park, Abingdon, Oxon, OX14 4RN

Routledge is an imprint of the Taylor & Francis Group, an informa business

© 2019 Taylor & Francis

The right of Susan B. Goldstein to be identified as author of this work
has been asserted by her in accordance with sections 77 and 78 of the
Copyright, Designs and Patents Act 1988.

First edition published by Pearson 2007
Second edition published by Routledge 2015

Library of Congress Cataloging-in-Publication Data
A catalog record has been requested for this book

ISBN: 978-0-367-18069-0 (hbk)
ISBN: 978-1-138-03708-3 (pbk)
ISBN: 978-0-429-19708-6 (ebk)

Typeset in Times New Roman
by Swales & Willis Ltd, Exeter, Devon, UK

Visit the eResources: www.routledge.com/9781138037083

CONTENTS

Preface

The Study of Culture and Psychology

Imagine that a visitor from another nation comes to your country to write a travel guide for his compatriots. He writes about various aspects of life that a traveler would need to understand, such as customs, food, transportation, and places to see. However, he gathers all of his information in one city and never travels to other areas of the country. Do you think people could rely on this guide to journey to areas outside of that city? In many ways this situation is analogous to research in the field of psychology. More than nine out of ten psychological studies are conducted in North America or Europe, areas that make up only about 12 percent of the world's population (Henrich, Heine, Norenzayan, 2010). This is a situation with serious consequences when culture-specific findings are erroneously assumed to be universal. For example, in health psychology the vast majority of studies on HIV/AIDS are conducted in the U.S., yet 98 percent of the world's AIDS deaths occur in southern Africa, with a markedly different pattern of infection (Arnett, 2008). In several of psychology's subfields, such as social psychology, research is conducted largely on U.S. undergraduate students in introductory psychology courses (Arnett, 2008; Henrich, Heine, Norenzayan, 2010). Yet these findings are often presented as if they apply to the behavior of all humans throughout the world. Not only are many research findings of questionable validity when applied outside of the regions where the studies were conducted, they are of questionable validity when applied uniformly *within* those regions. This is due to biases in psychological theory and research that result from the failure to acknowledge diversity associated with gender, ethnicity, social class, age, sexual orientation, and disability as well as the ways that these multiple identities interact to shape one's experiences (Cole, 2009). Thus, just as we may be misled by using the travel guide described above to negotiate through diverse regions of your country, we may also be misled by using "mainstream" psychological research to understand the diversity of human behavior.

It is only in recent decades that psychology as an academic discipline has begun to recognize the importance of a cultural perspective. When I finished graduate school and began interviewing for college teaching positions in the early 1990s, I found I often had to explain to potential employers what it meant to be trained in cross-cultural psychology (in fact, one department chair asked if my background prepared me to teach parapsychology – the study of psychic phenomena!). While cultural perspectives still remain somewhat marginalized in the field of psychology (Nielsen, Haun, Kärtner, & Legare, 2017), they have clearly gained a more central role in recent years. More colleges and universities are offering courses in cross-cultural psychology or have revised courses in traditional areas of psychology so as to be more inclusive of a cultural perspective. Authors of textbooks across the psychology curriculum have made corresponding changes with a greater focus on the role of culture in understanding human behavior. This book was designed to contribute to the inclusion of cultural perspectives in the psychology curriculum by providing students with hands-on experiences that facilitate the understanding and application of major concepts and principles in the study of culture and psychology.

Psychologists have taken a number of approaches to studying the role of culture in human behavior and many employ a combination of these perspectives:

Cross-cultural psychology focuses on comparing specific behaviors across cultures. For example, Stéphanie Laconi and colleagues (2018) surveyed individuals in nine European countries to investigate gender and cultural differences in Problematic Internet Use, sometimes called "Internet addiction." Cross-cultural psychologists work within a wide variety of research areas including social, developmental, cognitive, clinical, and organizational psychology. Rather than being characterized by a distinct content area, cross-cultural psychology is identified by the unique methods used to make comparisons across cultures, methods that are used to strive toward identifying universal principles of human behavior.

Cultural psychology focuses on detailing the interrelationships among forms of behavior within a specific culture and is generally less concerned with cross-cultural comparisons and the use of quantitative research methods. An example of this approach to culture and psychology is Barbara Rogoff's in-depth investigations of Mayan children's family and community interactions and learning processes (e.g., Rogoff et al., 2017). Cultural psychologists often use observational techniques as well as interviews to gather information about the beliefs and practices of a specific group.

The *indigenous psychologies* approach utilizes concepts and methods that arise from within the culture of interest (Kim, Yang, & Hwang, 2006). Pawel Boski (2006), for example, has described a form of indigenous psychology in Poland derived from a Catholic, noble-agrarian heritage that emphasizes humanism and anti-materialism.

Multicultural psychology, which grew from what is sometimes termed *ethnic psychology*, is concerned with the use of culturally appropriate methods to understand the behavior and experiences of people in culturally diverse environments and has focused primarily on historically marginalized groups in North America. For example, one recent study detailed the family social support networks of African American and Black Caribbean adolescents (Cross, Taylor, & Chatters, 2018).

Psychological anthropology involves anthropological studies that make explicit and systematic use of psychological methods and concepts (Bock, 1995). For example, Paula Tallman (2018) conducted ethnographic fieldwork with the Awajún community of the Peruvian Amazon to investigate how traditional markers of prestige had been replace by Western indicators of status based on occupation, income, education and Spanish-language use.

The majority of activities in this book are derived from the fields of cross-cultural, cultural, and multicultural psychology, although research findings from indigenous psychology and psychological anthropology are also represented. I hope that as you progress through the activities in this book you will gain a better understanding of how each of these approaches has contributed to our knowledge of the role of culture in human behavior.

References

Arnett, J. J. (2008). The neglected 95%: Why American psychology needs to become less American. *American Psychologist, 63*(7), 602–614.

Bock, P. K. (1995). *Rethinking psychological anthropology: Continuity and change in the study of human action.* Prospect Heights, IL: Waveland Press.

Boski, P. (2006). Humanism-materialism: Century-long Polish cultural origins and twenty years of research in cultural psychology. In U. Kim, K.-S. Yang, & K.-K. Hwang (Eds.), *Indigenous and cultural psychology: Understanding people in context* (pp. 373–402). New York: Springer.

Cole, E. R. (2009). Intersectionality and research in psychology. *American Psychologist, 64*(3), 170–180.

Cross, C. J., Taylor, R. J., & Chatters, L. M. (2018). Family social support networks of African American and Black Caribbean adolescents. *Journal of Child and Family Studies, 27,* 2757–2771.

Henrich, J., Heine, S. J., & Norenzayan, A. (2010). The weirdest people in the world? *Behavioral and Brain Sciences, 33* (2–3), 61–83.

Kim, U., Yang, K.-S., & Hwang, K.-K. (Eds.). (2006). *Indigenous and cultural psychology: Understanding people in context.* New York: Springer.

Laconi, S., Kaliszewska-Czeremska, K., Gnisci, A., Sergi, I., Barke, A., Jeromin, F., Groth, J., Gamez-Guadix, M., Keser Ozcan, N., Demetrovics, Z., Király, O., Siomos, K., Floros, G., & Kuss, D. J. (2018). Cross-cultural study of problematic internet use in nine European countries. *Computers in Human Behavior, 84,* 430–440.

Nielsen, M., Haun, D., Kärtner, J., & Legare, C. H. (2017). The persistent sampling bias in developmental psychology: A call to action. *Journal of Experimental Child Psychology, 162,* 31–38.

Rogoff, B., Coppens, A. D., Alcalá, L., Aceves-Azuara, I., Ruvalcaba, O., López, A., & Dayton, A. (2017). Noticing learners' strengths through cultural research. *Perspectives on Psychological Science, 12*(5), 876–888.

Tallman, P. (2018). "Now we live for the money": Shifting markers of status, stress, and immune function in the Peruvian Amazon. *Ethos.* Advance online publication. doi:10.1111/etho.12189

The Content and Structure of This Book

The activities that compose this book revolve around case studies, self-administered scales, mini-experiments, and the collection of content-analytic, observational, and interview data. Background material is included for any concepts not commonly addressed in introductory texts.

In this book, I have chosen to use a broad conceptualization of culture, inclusive of groups identified on a variety of dimensions in addition to nationality or race/ethnicity. This expanded view of culture and psychology reflects current thinking among cross-cultural scholars and allows for a discussion of culture in a context more relevant to the lives of many student readers.

The book is organized in terms of nine chapters of ten activities each, representing major content areas in research on culture and psychology:

- Chapter 1, The Concept of Culture, addresses the definition of culture and some basic dimensions on which cultures differ.
- Chapter 2, Culture and Psychological Research, explores major issues and techniques in the conduct of cross-cultural research.
- Chapter 3, Culture and Basic Processes, brings a cross-cultural perspective to the processes of cognition, memory, perception, and language.
- Chapter 4, Culture and Developmental Processes, focuses on socialization in cultural context and cultural variation in developmental processes.
- Chapter 5, Personality, Emotion, and the Self in Cultural Context, addresses the impact of culture on the construal of self, the expression of emotion across cultures, and the cross-cultural relevance of Western personality theory.
- Chapter 6, Health, Stress, and Coping across Cultures, deals with major issues in cross-cultural research on physical and mental well-being.
- Chapter 7, Culture and Social Behavior, explores major research findings in the areas of norms and values, conflict resolution, work-related behavior, close interpersonal relationships, gender roles, and the impact of technology on social behavior.
- Chapter 8, Intergroup Relations, explores the phenomena of prejudice, discrimination, stereotyping, and marginalization.
- Chapter 9, Intercultural Interaction, deals with research on intercultural communication, adjustment, and training.

You will also find an appendix at the end of the book that includes a variety of resources to assist you in exploring culture and psychology. These include Internet resources, graduate programs in culture and psychology, scholarly journals, professional associations, and social justice organizations. I hope that this appendix will serve as a useful reference as you approach the activities in this book as well as for cross-cultural pursuits outside of this course.

New to the Third Edition

In the years since the second edition of this book was published, the need for intercultural competence and awareness has become even more crucial as international conflicts erupt throughout the world, migration surges, and technological innovations make communicating across and within cultures more frequent and immediate. I have attempted to reflect these changes in this new edition as activities were substantially updated, and others were revised or replaced. Entirely new activities address such topics as cultural neuroscience, the global obesity epidemic, cultural syndromes of distress, anti-immigrant prejudice, the effect of geographic knowledge on intergroup attitudes, and the mental health consequences of climate change. You will also find that the resources in the appendix (as well as the Instructor's Manual) are substantially updated and expanded.

To the Student

Since I began teaching Introductory Psychology and Cross-Cultural Psychology nearly three decades ago, I have enjoyed devising new ways to involve my students in the exploration of culture and psychology. The activities in this book are a result of these efforts. I hope that you will find these activities exciting and challenging, that they provide you with a new perspective on human behavior, and that they help you to understand the role of culture in your own experiences and behaviors. Please read the instructions included in each activity carefully. Some of the activities involve collecting data from others and have specific directions regarding ethical considerations, such as maintaining confidentiality. Many of the activities have been modified in response to the feedback I received from my own students over the years. I would very much appreciate hearing from you about your experiences with these activities as well. You will find my e-mail address below.

To the Instructor

I often hear psychology instructors commenting on the difficulty of creating active learning experiences exploring cultural perspectives in psychology. Unlike other areas of psychology, one cannot easily ask students to replicate cross-cultural studies. Instead, this activity book provides students with a cross-cultural perspective through exploring their own cultural background, interviewing others with specific cross-cultural experiences, making cross-cultural comparisons using a broad interpretation of culture, and reading about cultures different from their own in library resources and the materials included in specific activities.

This book is designed for use as a supplement to courses specifically focusing on culture and human behavior, such as a cross-cultural psychology course, and as a means to integrate cultural perspectives into an introductory psychology course. The nine chapters represent the topics addressed in most cross-cultural psychology textbooks and correspond to the organization of most introductory psychology texts as well.

The large number of activities included in this book allows you to select those best suited to your course. Since the activities address thought-provoking issues and require that students engage in critical thinking, they may be assigned prior to class or during class to be used as the basis for class discussion. Several of the activities would be appropriate as small group projects. Students can either complete the activity as a group or bring the completed activity to class and work in a group to evaluate the pooled data. Since the activities are available to students in pdf form, they may be easily collected by instructors as individual assignments. Each of the activities may be assigned independently and out of sequence.

The instructor's manual that accompanies this book provides detailed suggestions on how to tailor specific activities to fit your course and is available online at www.routledge.com/9781138037083. It includes ideas for using the activities with more advanced students and for expanding the writing component of activities to include techniques drawn from the literature on writing across the curriculum, such as free writing, journaling, and peer review. The instructor's manual also includes a variety of lecture and discussion ideas, and video, text, and Internet materials relevant to specific activities in this book. As in my message to the students, I invite you to contact me with any feedback about your experiences with the activities. I hope you will find this book to be a helpful tool in guiding students through an exploration of the role of culture in human behavior.

Acknowledgments

I have many people to thank for their generous assistance with this book, including editor Carolyn Merrill and editorial assistants Lara Zeises and Amy Goldmacher on the first edition, editors Karon Bowers and Stephen Frail and editorial assistant Allison Rowland on the second edition, and editor Georgette Enriquez and editorial assistant Brian Eschrich on the third edition. My thinking about these activities was guided by the candid feedback of my students at the University of Redlands, and helpful suggestions from the reviewers: John Adamopoulos, Grand Valley State University; Karen L. Butler, Johnson C. Smith University; Susan E. Dutch, Westfield State College; G. William Hill, Kennesaw State University; James M. Jones, University of Delaware; Frank F. Montalvo, University of Texas – San Antonio; Connie Schick, Bloomsburg University, Yvonne Wells, Suffolk University; and Evangeline Wheeler, Towson University, on the first edition, Christine Bachman, University of Houston; Dawna K. Coutant, University of Hawaii at Hilo; David C. Devonis, Graceland University; and William R. Woodward, University of New Hampshire, on the second edition, and Dawn K. Kriebel and Michael Bender on the third edition. My thanks also go out to Sandi Richey, University of Redlands Interlibrary Loan Librarian, who worked miracles to obtain books and articles from across the globe. I would not have been able to complete this book without the unending patience and encouragement of my husband, Paul, who, for over three decades, has been my best friend and most valued source of perspective. Finally, I am thankful to my wonderful daughters, Lauren and Rachel, who have helped me to understand the need for all of us to embark upon cross-cultural explorations.

Susan B. Goldstein
Department of Psychology, University of Redlands
1200 East Colton Avenue, P.O. Box 3080
Redlands, CA 92373
E-mail: susan_goldstein@redlands.edu

The Concept of Culture

ACTIVITY 1.1
IS PSYCHOLOGY CULTURE BOUND?

Psychology as a discipline strives to identify and describe universal principles of behavior. However, most psychological research has been conducted with undergraduate students in "WEIRD" (**W**estern, **E**ducated, **I**ndustrialized, **R**ich, and **D**emocratic) societies, one of the least representative populations for drawing conclusions about human behavior (Henrich, Heine, & Norenzayan, 2010). Unfortunately, many psychology textbooks discuss these research findings as if they are universal, even in cases where cross-cultural studies indicate otherwise. This activity asks you to think about several concepts that appear in introductory psychology textbooks and consider the universality of each.

Directions: Read the description of each of the psychological concepts below. Then indicate in the space provided after each concept whether you believe it applies to all people (universal) or believe it is limited to certain cultural groups (culture-specific). Write a brief explanation of your response. When you are finished you can check your answers at the back of this book.

1. *Susceptibility to visual illusions* – Although the two lines in the Müller-Lyer illusion below are the same length, the second line with the reverse arrowheads looks longer.

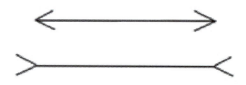

2. *The serial-position effect (primacy and recency)* – The first few items and the last few items in a list are remembered better than the items in the middle of the list.

---

3. *Social loafing* – The tendency for people to exert less effort when working as a group than when individually accountable.

4. *Secure attachment* – Mary Ainsworth and colleagues (1978) delineated three types of attachment: secure, avoidant, and ambivalent. Secure attachment is viewed as ideal in terms of the development of basic trust and other mental health indices (Waters, Merrick, Treboux, Crowell, & Albersheim, 2003).

5. *Delusions and hallucinations* – Delusions and hallucinations are signs of mental illness, specifically schizophrenia.

6. *Self-serving bias* – The tendency to use dispositional (internal) attributions when explaining our successes and situational (external) attributions when explaining our failures.

7. *Pain perception* – Pain is an unpleasant sensory experience conveyed to the brain by neurons, which signals actual or potential tissue damage.

References

Ainsworth, M. D. S., Blehar, M. D., Waters, E., & Wall, S. (1978). *Patterns of attachment: A psychological study of the Strange Situation*. Hillsdale, NJ: Lawrence Erlbaum.

Henrich, J., Heine, S. J., & Norenzayan, A. (2010). The weirdest people in the world? *Behavioral and Brain Sciences, 33* (2–3), 111–135.

Waters, E., Merrick, S., Treboux, D., Crowell, J., & Albersheim, L. (2003). Attachment security in infancy and early adulthood: A twenty-year longitudinal study. In M. E. Herzig & E. A. Farber (Eds.), *Annual progress in child psychiatry and child development* (pp. 63–72). New York, NY: Brunner-Routledge.

ACTIVITY 1.2
WHAT IS CULTURE?

Culture is not an easy concept to define. Even among those who study culture and human behavior there are a large number of definitions in use. Perhaps the most straightforward definition is that of Melville Herskovits (1948) who proposed that culture is the human-made part of the environment. Harry Triandis and colleagues (1972) further suggested that culture has both physical components (such as tools, buildings, and works of art) and subjective components (such as roles, values, and attitudes). Recently, the term *culture* has been used more broadly to refer to the common values, beliefs, and behaviors within groups that share an ethnic heritage, disability, sexual orientation, or socioeconomic class, as well as to those who share a corporate identity, occupation, sport, or college campus. This activity encourages you to explore the meaning of culture by applying several commonly cited criteria (e.g., Baldwin, Faulkner, Hecht, & Lindsley, 2005; Matsumoto & Hwang, 2013) to determine whether a specific group is, in fact, a culture.

Directions: Identify a group that you think of as having its own culture. First describe this group, then by answering the questions below, decide whether this group has the characteristics of a culture.

Group Name and Description:

1. Does the group hold shared perspectives, norms, values, or assumptions that direct the behavior of its members? Please give an example.

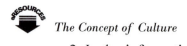

2. Is the information that is important to this group learned and handed down through generations (or cohorts) of its members? Please give an example.

3. Does this group have a common language, dialect, or set of terms? Please give an example.

4. Are the perspectives and practices of this group widely shared among its members? Please give an example.

5. Do members react strongly when the perspectives or practices of this group are not upheld? Please give an example.

6. Do the practices of this group contribute to its survival and the well-being of its members? Please give an example.

7. Discuss your conclusions about whether the group you chose to examine is a culture.

Thinking Further

1. Is it helpful to distinguish cultures from subcultures? Why or why not?

2. There has been criticism of cross-cultural research that equates culture with nationality and makes comparisons between members of different countries (e.g., Italians and Canadians). What might there be concern about this approach?

3. How might culture be distinguished from race, ethnicity, and nationality?

References

Baldwin, J. R., Faulkner, S. L., Hecht, M. L., & Lindsley, S. L. (Eds.). (2005). *Redefining culture: Perspectives across the disciplines*. Hillsdale, NJ: Lawrence Erlbaum Associates.

Herskovits, M. J. (1948). *Man and his works: The science of cultural anthropology*. New York, NY: Knopf.

Matsumoto, D., & Hwang, H. S. (2013). Culture. In K. Keith (Ed.), *Encyclopedia of cross-cultural psychology* (pp. 345–347). London, UK: Wiley-Blackwell.

Triandis, H. C., Vassiliou, V., Vassiliou, G., Tanaka, Y., & Shanmugam, A. V. (1972). *The analysis of subjective culture*. New York, NY: Wiley.

ACTIVITY 1.3
HUMAN UNIVERSALS

One criticism of research on culture and psychology is that it focuses too much on cultural differences and neglects similarities. This may be due to several factors including the statistical methods used in psychological research, which are aimed at testing for differences, and an innate tendency of humans to categorize others into groups (Lalonde, Cila, Lou, & Cribbie, 2015). Another reason for this focus on differences may be that it is very difficult to determine criteria for establishing universals. For example, Ara Norenzayan and Steven Heine (2005) differentiated between types of universals that depend on whether a phenomenon exists across cultures, is used to solve the same problems across cultures, and is equally accessible to individuals in those cultures. This activity encourages you to consider similarities across cultures and their importance to our understanding of human behavior.

Directions: In his book on human universals, anthropologist Donald E. Brown (1991) presented a description of the *Universal People* (or UPs) as a means of explaining commonalities across cultures, societies, and language groups. For example, Brown suggested that the UPs have a language that allows them to think and speak about things that are not physically present, they have childhood fears, they distinguish right from wrong, they have specific standards of attractiveness and so on. In the space below, write a paragraph or two describing additional characteristics of the Universal People. What characteristics do all humans share? Some aspects you might address in your description of the UPs include language, emotions, self-concept, daily activities, social interaction, family and community structure, rituals, and view of outsiders.

Thinking Further

1. Human universals nearly always aid survival in some way (Buss, 2001). They can be innate psychological tendencies, such as the ability to learn languages, or learned behaviors in response to human needs, such as counting systems (Norenzayan & Heine, 2005). Human universals may also reflect physical facts, such as a preference for right handedness, which is common across cultures (Brown, 2004). Choose one of the universals you identified in your description of the Universal People and discuss possible sources of that universal (innate psychological tendency, learned behavior in response to human needs, reflection of physical facts, or other sources).

2. What might be some of the costs of focusing on differences rather than similarities in research on culture and psychology? Please explain.

References

Brown, D. E. (1991). *Human universals*. Philadelphia, PA: Temple University Press.

Brown, D. E. (2004). Human universals, human nature & human culture. *Daedalus*, *133*(4), 47–54.

Buss, D. M. (2001). Human nature and culture: An evolutionary psychological perspective. *Journal of Personality*, *69*(6), 955–978.

Lalonde R. N., Cila J., Lou E., & Cribbie, R. A. (2015). Are we really that different from each other? The difficulties of focusing on similarities in cross-cultural research. *Peace and Conflict: Journal of Peace Psychology*, *21*(4), 525–534.

Norenzayan, A., & Heine, S. J. (2005). Psychological universals: What are they and how can we know? *Psychological Bulletin*, *131*(5), 763–784.

ACTIVITY 1.4
CROSS-CULTURAL PSYCHOLOGY'S DEATH WISH

Walter Lonner (2018, p. 82) suggested that culture-oriented psychology has a "death wish" in that it strives to no longer exist as a separate field of psychology once cross-cultural perspectives become "a central and commonplace component of psychological thinking, research, and application." This activity will allow you to investigate how close psychology has come to making this wish come true.

Directions: First, find a university-level textbook on a specific subtopic in psychology (e.g., research methods, biopsychology, states of consciousness, sensation and perception, lifespan development, motivation and emotion, learning, memory, cognition, gender and sexuality, health psychology, personality, social psychology, psychological disorders, therapy). You may also use a specific chapter of an introduction to psychology textbook (some complete textbooks are available online). Then answer the questions below.

1. State the author, title and topic of the textbook or chapter you selected.

2. List and briefly describe the concepts or theories for which cultural perspectives have been included in the chapter or textbook.

---

3. Discuss at least one topic in the chapter or text where you believe a cultural perspective is necessary but has been omitted.

Thinking further

What changes over time do you think will facilitate the integration of cultural perspectives across areas of psychology?

Reference

Lonner, W. J. (2018). The continuing growth of cross-cultural psychology: A first-person, annotated chronology. In Keith, K. D. (Ed.), *Elements in psychology and culture* (pp. 1–92). New York, NY: Cambridge University Press.

ACTIVITY 1.5
A SEARCH FOR INDIVIDUALISM AND COLLECTIVISM

The concepts of individualism and collectivism have received great attention in research on culture and psychology and continue to be debated and revised (e.g., Minkov et al., 2017; Taras et al., 2014). These terms stem from Hofstede's (1980) classic cross-cultural study of workplace values. According to Hofstede (2001, p. 225),

> Individualism stands for a society in which the ties between individuals are loose; everyone is expected to look after him/herself and her/his immediate family only. Collectivism stands for a society in which people from birth onwards are integrated into strong cohesive in-groups, which throughout people's lifetime continue to protect them in exchange for unquestioning loyalty.

This activity encourages you to explore these concepts by seeking out real-life examples of individualism and collectivism.

Directions: Reread the definitions of individualism and collectivism above. Then identify one real-life example of individualism and one of collectivism (such as a behavior, an object, a song, or an advertising slogan). The ease with which you can find these examples will depend on whether you live in a more individualistic or collectivistic culture. However, you should be able to find some forms of collectivism within an individualistic culture and some forms of individualism within a collectivistic culture. Examples of individualism might include an advertisement for an electric blanket that has separate settings for the right and left sides or a brochure for a preschool curriculum in which activities depend on the individual child's skills and interests. Examples of collectivism might include information on a community bicycle-sharing program or a T-shirt imprinted with the insignia of your university. If possible, bring your examples to class with this completed assignment.

1. Describe your example of individualism and explain why it illustrates individualism.

2. Describe your example of collectivism and explain why it illustrates collectivism.

Thinking Further

1. Studies show that greater cross-cultural differences in individualism and collectivism are expressed in "cultural products," such as those you and your classmates collected, than in self-ratings of behaviors, beliefs, or feelings (Morling, 2016; Morling & Lamoreaux, 2008). Why might that be so? [Hint: Consider the *source* of those cultural products.]

2. Cultural values are not static but change over time. After analyzing 51 years of data from 78 countries, Henri Santos, Michael Varnum, and Igor Grossman (2017) reported that individualism is increasing and appears to accompany a country's socioeconomic development. How might you explain this finding?

3. Cultural dimensions such as individualism and collectivism can help us to "unpackage" cross-cultural research findings. For example, in England relatives of people with drug and alcohol problems were found to be more likely to cope with stress by withdrawing from others than were their counterparts in Mexico (Orford et al., 2001). How might it be helpful to know that England is considered a more individualist society and Mexico is considered a more collectivist society? What are the limitations of attributing these differences in coping to differences in individualism and collectivism, particularly since we have only two countries to compare?

References

Hofstede, G. (1980). *Culture's consequences: International differences in work-related values*. Beverly Hills, CA: Sage.

Hofstede, G (2001). *Culture's consequences: Comparing values, behaviors, and organizations across nations* (2nd ed.). Beverly Hills, CA: Sage.

Minkov, M., Dutt, P., Schachner, M., Morales, O., Sanchez, C., Jandosova, J., Khassenbekov, Y., & Mudd, B. (2017). A revision of Hofstede's individualism-collectivism dimension: A new national index from a 56-country study. *Cross Cultural & Strategic Management, 24*(3), 386–404.

Morling, B. (2016). Cultural difference, inside and out. *Social and Personality Psychology Compass, 10*(12), 693–706.

Morling, B., & Lamoreaux, M. (2008). Measuring culture outside the head: A meta-analysis of individualism-collectivism in cultural products. *Personality and Social Psychology Review, 12*(3), 199–221.

Orford, J., Natera, G., Velleman, R., Copello, A., Bowie, N., Bradbury, C., Davies, J., Mora, J., Nava, A., Rigby, K., & Tiburcio, M. (2001). Ways of coping and the health of relatives facing drug and alcohol problems in Mexico and England. *Addiction, 96*(5), 761–774.

Santos, H. C., Varnum, M. E. W., & Grossmann, I. (2017). Global increases in individualism. *Psychological Science, 28*(9), 1228–1239.

Taras, V., Sarala, R., Muchinsky, P., Kemmelmeier, M., Singelis, T. M., Avsec, A., . . . Sinclair, H. C. (2014). Opposite ends of the same stick? Multi-method test of the dimensionality of individualism and collectivism. *Journal of Cross-Cultural Psychology, 45*(2), 213–245.

ACTIVITY 1.6
CLEANLINESS BELIEFS

One of the complaints sojourners often have when they visit another culture is that cleanliness practices are not adequate. This activity will help you to explore your own cleanliness beliefs and put them in cross-cultural perspective.

Directions: Respond to the items below to indicate your cleanliness beliefs.

1. People in my culture value cleanliness.

STRONGLY DISAGREE						STRONGLY AGREE
1	2	3	4	5	6	7

Please explain:

2. One should wash one's body before entering a bathtub full of clean water.

STRONGLY DISAGREE						STRONGLY AGREE
1	2	3	4	5	6	7

3. Blankets and rugs should be hung out daily to air.

STRONGLY DISAGREE						STRONGLY AGREE
1	2	3	4	5	6	7

4. Shoes should be removed before entering a home.

STRONGLY DISAGREE						STRONGLY AGREE
1	2	3	4	5	6	7

5. The left hand should not be used for eating or taking food from communal dishes.

STRONGLY DISAGREE						STRONGLY AGREE
1	2	3	4	5	6	7

6. One should shower or bathe daily.

STRONGLY DISAGREE						STRONGLY AGREE
1	2	3	4	5	6	7

7. Cleaning products should be used in the home to kill germs.

STRONGLY DISAGREE						STRONGLY AGREE
1	2	3	4	5	6	7

8. Hands should be washed upon returning home.

STRONGLY DISAGREE						STRONGLY AGREE
1	2	3	4	5	6	7

9. One should blow one's nose into the gutter rather than carry the mucus in a cloth or tissue.

STRONGLY DISAGREE						STRONGLY AGREE
1	2	3	4	5	6	7

10. The toilet should not be located under the same roof as the place where people eat and prepare food or sleep.

STRONGLY DISAGREE						STRONGLY AGREE
1	2	3	4	5	6	7

Thinking Further

1. Look over your answers to the questions above. With which cleanliness practices did you AGREE most strongly? What cultural messages were you taught that support these practices?

2. With which practices did you DISAGREE most strongly? What cultural messages were you taught that conflict with these practices?

3. What other cleanliness practices not listed above are important to you?

4. Review your responses above. Are there any of your cleanliness beliefs that could be considered poor hygiene by someone from a culture other than your own?

5. Look back at your response to item 1. Is there anything you would like to add or change in your answer?

Sources

Cleanliness belief items are based on the following articles:

Fernea, E., & Fernea, R. A. (1994). Cleanliness and culture. In W. J. Lonner & R. S. Malpass (Eds.), *Psychology and culture* (pp. 65–70). Boston, MA: Allyn & Bacon.
Waxler-Morrison, N., Anderson, J., & Richardson, E. (1990). *Cross-cultural caring: A handbook for health professionals in Western Canada*. Vancouver, BC: University of British Columbia Press.

ACTIVITY 1.7
CULTURAL METAPHORS

Despite the large amount of information researchers have gathered about different cultures, it is often difficult to convey to others exactly what a specific culture is like. Yoshihisa Kashima (1994) explained that metaphors may allow us to more easily grasp a new concept by framing it in terms of something familiar. Martin Gannon (e.g., Gannon, 2004; Gannon, & Pillai, 2010) proposed the use of *cultural metaphors* as a way to easily express a cultural mindset and compare it to that of other cultures. These metaphors involve identifying an activity or phenomenon that most members of a culture would view as important, and then using it as a metaphor for describing key features of the cultural group. While cultural metaphors are generalizations and will not apply to all members of a group, they can provide a framework for beginning to understand and compare cultural groups. For example, Margaret Phillips and colleagues (2012, p. 284) described how the ackee fruit serves as a metaphor for understanding the Jamaican national culture and business environment. They focused on four stages of the ackee's development and use: the tree, the closed fruit, the open/ripe fruit, and the cooked fruit:

- The hardiness of the tree symbolizes the "intrinsic resilience" of the Jamaican people that allows for optimism and the ability to overcome challenging environmental conditions.
- The temporarily poisonous closed fruit reflects the "transitional toxicity" of the social and economic dysfunction that occurs due to the current stage of development of the Jamaican economy and political system.
- The open/ripe fruit, which is colorful, serves multiple functions, and is dependent upon integration with other ingredients, represents the "multifaceted diversity" of Jamaican society, with its ethnic diversity, creative resourcefulness, and cooperative relationships with foreign influences.
- The communal experience of consuming the cooked fruit reflects a "ritualistic identity" that promotes pride and cohesion in Jamaican society.

The purpose of this activity is to familiarize you with the concept of cultural metaphor and provide you with an experience constructing such metaphors.

Directions: Construct your own metaphor for a culture with which you are familiar. Gannon (2009) cautioned that much thought is required to avoid inaccurate stereotyping. You may select a culture based on nationality or may conceptualize culture more broadly to include other groups based on such dimensions as social class or ethnicity. You may even construct a metaphor to convey the essence of a student organization or sports team. Choose four or five dimensions of the culture

to describe through your metaphor. Some suggestions for dimensions you might address include:

- basic values
- communication style
- gender roles
- key events, holidays or activities
- methods of socialization

- rules for social interaction
- social structure
- stressors and coping mechanisms
- view of cultural outsiders
- work-related values

In the space provided below, describe the culture you have selected and explain your cultural metaphor in some detail.

Source

Based on Phillips, M. E., Scott, A. D., Sutherland, C. E., Gerla, M. P., & Gilzene, A. M. (2012). Carry mi ackee go a Jamaican market: Ackee as a metaphor for the organization and environment of Jamaican business. *International Journal of Cross Cultural Management, 12*(3), 277–297. Copyright © 2012 by Sage. Adapted with permission.

References

Gannon, M. J. (2004). *Understanding global cultures: Metaphorical journeys through 28 nations, clusters of nations, and continents* (3rd ed.). Thousand Oaks, CA: Sage.

Gannon, M. J. (2009). The cultural metaphoric method: Description, analysis, and critique. *International Journal of Cross Cultural Management, 9*(3), 275–287.

Gannon, M., & Pillai, R. (2010). *Understanding global cultures: metaphorical journeys through 29 nations, clusters of nations, continents, and diversity.* Thousand Oaks, CA: Sage.

Kashima, Y. (1994) Cultural metaphors of the mind and the organization. In A.-M. Bouvy, F. J. R. van de Vijver, P. Boski, & P. Schmitz (Eds.), *Journeys into cross-cultural psychology: Selected papers from the eleventh international conference of the International Association for Cross-Cultural Psychology* (pp. 351–363). Amsterdam: Swets & Zeitlinger.

Phillips, M. E., Scott, A. D., Sutherland, C. E., Gerla, M. P., & Gilzene, A. M. (2012). Carry mi ackee go a Jamaican market: Ackee as a metaphor for the organization and environment of Jamaican business. *International Journal of Cross Cultural Management, 12*(3), 277–297.

ACTIVITY 1.8
ETHNOCENTRISM, CULTURAL RELATIVISM, AND UNIVERSAL HUMAN RIGHTS

When we encounter cultural practices or beliefs that differ from our own, there are several approaches we can take. An *ethnocentric* approach uses the standards of one's own culture to judge the practices of people from other cultures. In contrast, a *cultural relativist* approach involves evaluating an individual's behaviors based on their own cultural context. Most researchers of culture have adopted a philosophy of cultural relativism to some extent but view as unacceptable cultural practices that violate *universal human rights*, such as the killing of women considered to have violated their family's honor (Woolf & Hulsizer, 2013). These concepts have important applications beyond the study of culture and psychology. For example, courts in many countries with multicultural populations are grappling with *cultural offense* cases in which an act viewed as appropriate among members of a specific subpopulation violates the laws of that country (Muzzica, Tamborra, & Amarelli, 2015). This activity encourages you to explore the complexities of applying the concepts of ethnocentrism, cultural relativism and universal rights.

Directions: For each of the incidents listed below, discuss your opinion and then indicate whether that opinion is driven by ethnocentrism, cultural relativism, or universal human rights.

1. A Quebec court has ruled that a 12-year old Sikh boy should be allowed to wear his ceremonial sword – known as a kirpan – while he is at school. For devout Sikh men, wearing the kirpan is an essential part of the religious faith. The decision overturned one made by his school, which banned him from carrying the small blunt metal dagger because they regarded it as a weapon.

    Do you believe the court made the correct decision? Is your response based on ethnocentrism, cultural relativism, or universal rights? Please explain.

2. In 1985, upon learning that her husband had a mistress, a Japanese woman living in the United States attempted parent–child suicide by walking into the

ocean with her two children. Her two children drowned in the attempt, but she survived and although she was charged with murder by the California Superior Court, she was convicted of the lesser a charge of voluntary manslaughter and sentenced to one year in prison. While illegal in Japan, this ancient Japanese custom, called *oyako-shinju* has tended to be treated with leniency since it is viewed as a means by which a family can avoid an otherwise unacceptable social predicament (Nambu, Nasu, Nishimura, & Fujiwara, 2011). *Oyako-shinju* is based on the traditional cultural belief that it is crueler to leave the children behind with no one to look after them than it is for the mother to take them with her to the afterlife.

Do you believe the court made the correct decision? Is your response based on ethnocentrism, cultural relativism, or universal rights? Please explain.

3. In 2017, the European Court of Justice ruled that employers have the right to stop employees from wearing visible religious symbols, including clothing (such as the burka and niqab) and headscarves (such as hijab) worn in the name of Islam.

Do you believe the European Court of Justice made the correct decision? Is your response based on ethnocentrism, cultural relativism, or universal rights? Please explain.

4. In 2005, King Abdulaziz University of Saudi Arabia paid Virginia Tech University $246,000 to design and operate summer courses for 60 of the King Abdulaziz faculty – courses that were held on the Virginia Tech campus. Following Saudi custom and the preferences of the King Abdulaziz University professors, the 30 female professors and 30 male professors were taught in

---

The Concept of Culture

separate classes. Several Virginia Tech faculty members objected, stating that this action violated federal anti-discrimination laws.

Do you believe that Virginia Tech made the correct decision? Is your response based on ethnocentrism, cultural relativism, or universal rights? Please explain.

5. Although bullfighting is illegal in the United States, a bullfighting academy has been operating in Southern California since 1996. Students at this school do not train with real animals, yet the San Diego County Humane Society opposes the school, which it views as promoting animal cruelty. One of the founders of the academy, however, takes the position that bullfighting is an important cultural practice and should not be prohibited.

Do you believe this school should be allowed to operate? Is your response based on ethnocentrism, cultural relativism, or universal human (or animal) rights? Please explain.

Thinking Further

Based on your answers to the questions above, write a brief statement explaining the conditions under which you believe it is justified to take an ethnocentric, cultural relativist, or universal rights perspective when considering the practices of cultures other than your own.

References

Muzzica, R., Tamborra, T. L., & Amarelli, G. (2015). Emerging cultural conflicts in Italy: A challenge for criminal law. *International Journal of Criminology and Sociology, 4,* 141–153.

Nambu, S., Nasu, A., Nishimura, S., & Fujiwara, S. (2011). Fatal child abuse in Japan: Does a trend exist toward tougher sentencing? *Journal of Injury and Violence Research, 3*(2), 74–79.

Woolf, L. M., & Hulsizer, M. R. (2013). Human rights. In K. Keith (Ed.), *Encyclopedia of cross-cultural psychology* (pp. 668–671). London, UK: Wiley-Blackwell.

ACTIVITY 1.9
EXPLORING THE WORLD VILLAGE

This activity, based on the format of The World Village Project, is designed to help you view the population of the world from a more global perspective.

Directions: Imagine a village of 100 people that represents the planet Earth. Answer the questions below, assuming that all of the human ratios in the village are the same as those of the world.

Of the 100 inhabitants, indicate how many would fall into each of the following categories. The correct answers are at the back of this book.

1. *Men and Women*
   _____ are men
   _____ are women

2. *Age*
   _____ are under age 15
   _____ are over age 65

3. *Places of Origin*
   _____ are Africans   _____ are South Americans
   _____ are Asians   _____ are North Americans
   _____ are Europeans   _____ are Oceanians (Australia, New
                                                    Zealand, Papua New Guinea)

4. *Primary Language*
   _____ speak Arabic   _____ speak Mandarin
   _____ speak Bengali   _____ speak Portuguese
   _____ speak English   _____ speak Punjabi
   _____ speak Hindi   _____ speak Russian
   _____ speak Japanese   _____ speak Spanish

5. *Religion*
   _____ are atheists   _____ are Muslims
   _____ are Buddhists   _____ are non-religious
   _____ are Christians   _____ are other religions
   _____ are Hindus

6. *Education*

_____ are illiterate adults

_____ are children without access to school

_____ hold a college degree

7. *Technology*

_____ have a cell phone

_____ have Internet access

_____ have cars

8. *Health and Well-being*

_____ have access to clean drinking water

_____ have a reliable source of food

_____ live in urban areas

_____ live in substandard housing

_____ lack access to toilets

_____ are refugees

_____ are affected by mental health problems

_____ live with a disability

_____ have HIV/AIDS

_____ smoke

_____ are obese

9. *Wealth*

_____ live below the internationally defined poverty line (less than U.S. $2 per day)

_____ control 85% of the world's money supply

ACTIVITY 1.10
A GLOBAL VIEW OF PSYCHOLOGY

Most of what is published in psychology journals and textbooks takes a *Western* perspective and ignores the psychologies that have been developed by scholars across the globe to address concerns relevant to their own cultures (sometimes labeled *indigenous psychology*). The purpose of this activity is twofold. First, it will acquaint you with some of the research interests of psychologists throughout the world. Second, it will encourage you to think about some of the forces that have shaped what is considered *Western psychology*.*

Directions: Read about the field of psychology in a country other than your own (one good source is the *Psychology International* newsletter of the American Psychological Association's International Affairs Office. Archived copies may be found at www.apa.org/international).

    1. Provide the complete citation for your article (see references at the end of activities in this book for examples of citation format and content).

    2. In a paragraph or two, describe below what you learned about the focus of psychology in the country you investigated.

*The term *Western psychology* can itself be viewed as ethnocentric in that it ignores the diverse cultures of the West and focuses only on those of European tradition.

3. What social, cultural, political, historical, environmental, economic, or religious factors may have shaped the research focus of psychology in the country you selected?

Thinking Further

Consider the theories, methods, and priorities of Western psychology. What do you conclude about the social, cultural, political, historical, environmental, economic, or religious factors that may have shaped its research focus? Please explain.

Culture and Psychological Research

ACTIVITY 2.1
FUNCTIONS OF CROSS-CULTURAL RESEARCH

As you have probably realized by now, cross-cultural research is not without its challenges. Efforts must be made to identify appropriate cultures for testing a theory and to develop or select measures and procedures that will ensure cross-cultural comparisons are based on equivalent data. Why, then, would social scientists make the effort to conduct such research? Researchers choose to conduct cross-cultural studies for many different reasons. The purpose of this activity is to become familiar with the major functions of cross-cultural research.

Directions: Several functions of cross-cultural research have been identified and described (Berry, Poortinga, Breugelmans, Chasiotis, & Sam, 2011; Brislin, 2000). Read the functions of cross-cultural research listed below. Then, for each of the research project descriptions that follow, indicate which of the functions is served by taking a cross-cultural approach. More than one function may be relevant to some of the project descriptions. Once you finish you can check your answers at the back of this book.

Functions of Cross-cultural Research

a. Identifying culture-specific values, cognitive categories, or forms of behavior.
b. Unconfounding variables. Two variables that may be linked in one culture may be unrelated in another culture.
c. Expanding the range of variables.
d. Understanding the relationship between ecological and psychological variables.
e. Investigating possible human universals.
f. Testing the generality of psychological models or theories.
g. Studying the effect of cultural change.

Project Descriptions

1. A Japanese expert on post-traumatic stress disorder constructed a model for predicting the likelihood that someone will develop psychological disturbances in response to extreme trauma. His original model was based on a study of survivors of the Fukushima earthquake and tsunami in Japan. He wondered if his model would also be a good predictor in other cultures, so he tested it on data from survivors of Hurricane Maria in Puerto Rico.

   What function was served by taking a cross-cultural approach? Please explain.

2. A community psychologist was interested in the effect of neighborhood stability on willingness to participate in community-based recycling programs. She was having some difficulty conducting her research because in her own country many neighborhoods had high residential mobility (people move homes frequently). By including several other countries in her study, she was able to explore "willingness to participate" within unstable, moderately stable, and highly stable neighborhoods.

    What function was served by taking a cross-cultural approach? Please explain.

3. A social psychologist was studying the impact of exposure to Internet content on children's beliefs about the value of material goods. In her own country, only wealthy families have Internet access, thus causing difficulty in separating the effects of Internet content from the effects of growing up in a wealthy family. Instead, she decided to conduct her research in Canada where she could find children with different levels of exposure to Internet content at both high- and low-income levels.

    What function was served by taking a cross-cultural approach? Please explain.

4. An experimental psychologist was interested in the effect of urban living on depth perception. He reasoned that city dwellers might be less sensitive than people in rural environments to depth cues that involve distance. He used stimuli to assess the perception of depth cues with individuals living in cultures based in a variety of urban and rural environments.

What function was served by taking a cross-cultural approach? Please explain.

5. An interdisciplinary team of researchers was exploring the reasons why members of certain ethnic groups were underrepresented as clients of a neighborhood mediation center. They hypothesized that the techniques used to resolve disputes at the mediation center may be culturally inappropriate for some groups of people. Instead of encouraging members of those groups to use the mediation center, they decided to conduct a cross-cultural study to identify methods of resolving disputes that were indigenous to those ethnic groups.

What function was served by taking a cross-cultural approach? Please explain.

6. A clinical psychologist was interested in the impact of exposure to Western values on eating disorders. He decided to investigate changes over time in rates of anorexia and bulimia in areas with growing exposure to Western media.

What function was served by taking a cross-cultural approach? Please explain.

7. A student of psychology read that in her own country boys outperformed girls in measures of mathematical achievement. She wondered if this might be due to biological sex differences and was found in all cultures or if it reflected differences in experience (such as educational or career opportunities). When she looked into the cross-cultural literature she found that in some countries researchers found gender differences in mathematical achievement scores and in others they did not.

What function was served by taking a cross-cultural approach? Please explain.

References

Berry, J. W., Poortinga, Y. H., Breugelmans, S. M., Chasiotis, A., & Sam, D. L. (2011). *Cross-cultural psychology: Research and applications* (3rd ed.). Cambridge, UK: Cambridge University Press.

Brislin, R. (2000). *Understanding culture's influence on behavior* (2nd ed.). Belmont, CA: Wadsworth.

ACTIVITY 2.2
INSIDERS AND OUTSIDERS

Psychologists have long emphasized objectivity in research and have expressed concern about bias stemming from the researcher being too close to the groups they are studying. In contrast, anthropologists have traditionally taken an approach that involves participating in the circumstances they are describing or analyzing. What are the advantages of being a cultural outsider or a cultural insider? This activity is designed to clarify differences between the insider perspective and the outsider perspective in conducting cross-cultural research.

Directions: Find an organized group or club that is well known on or off your campus. Identify two people to interview about this group: one who is a member (an insider) and one who has heard something about the group but is not a member (an outsider). Ask the same questions outlined below to both interviewees. Please assure your respondents that their identities will remain confidential. Do not include their names on these sheets.

Group: _____

Interview A: Insider (Member)

1. How did you first learn about this group?

2. What are the criteria for membership?

3. How would you characterize the members of this group?

4. What are the goals of this group?

5. How effective is this group in achieving their goals? Please explain.

6. What is the perception most nonmembers have of this group?

Interview B: Outsider (Nonmember)

1. How did you first learn about this group?

2. What are the criteria for membership?

3. How would you characterize the members of this group?

4. What are the goals of this group?

5. How effective is this group in achieving their goals? Please explain.

6. What is the perception most nonmembers have of this group?

First compare the responses from the two interviews, then answer the questions below.

1. Describe the major differences between the two accounts.

2. What are the advantages and disadvantages of using insiders as an information source?

3. What are the advantages and disadvantages of using outsiders as an information source?

Thinking Further

What would you recommend for cross-cultural psychologists in terms of being an insider or outsider relative to the cultures they study?

ACTIVITY 2.3
EMIC AND ETIC PERSPECTIVES

The purpose of this activity is to familiarize you with a key concept in studying culture and human behavior; the distinction between *emics* and *etics*. According to John Berry (1969), etic research takes an outsider's perspective and focuses on the search for human universals, whereas emic research takes an insider's perspective and addresses the way behaviors are expressed within a specific culture. Berry warned us about the danger of an *imposed etic* in which we assume that research concepts or methodologies developed in one culture have the same meaning across cultural groups. For example, people in all cultures make moral judgments, but a study that employs measures of Kohlberg's stages of moral development across cultures is using an imposed etic. Instead, it may be possible to identify emic forms of moral behavior, such as *ahimsa*, an Indian principle of nonviolence based on respect for all life (Eckensberger & Zimba, 1997). Cross-cultural research should ideally lead to *derived etics*, based on common features of emic phenomena (Berry, Poortinga, Breugelmans, Chasiotis, & Sam, 2011).

Directions: First add five etics to the list below. Then choose one of these etics, select a cultural group with which you are familiar, and describe an associated emic for that cultural group. For example, "social relationships" is an etic category, but the Chinese concept of *guanxi* addresses an emic aspect of social relationships, "the closeness of a relationship that is associated with a particular set of differentiated behavioral obligations based on social and ethical norms" (Mao, Peng, & Wong, 2012, p. 1161).

Etics

a. childrearing practices   f. _____

b. gender roles   g. _____

c. leadership   h. _____

d. humor   i. _____

e. expression of emotion   j. _____

1. Identify the etic you selected.

---

2. Describe an associated emic.

References

Berry, J. W. (1969). On cross-cultural comparability. *International Journal of Psychology, 4*, 119–128.

Berry, J. W., Poortinga, Y. H., Breugelmans, S. M., Chasiotis, A., & Sam, D. L. (2011). *Cross-cultural psychology: Research and applications* (3rd ed.). New York, NY: Cambridge University Press.

Eckensberger, L. H., & Zimba, R. F. (1997). The development of moral judgment. In J. W. Berry, P. R. Dasen, & T. S. Saraswathi (Eds.), *Handbook of cross-cultural psychology: Vol. 2. Basic processes and human development* (2nd ed., pp. 299–338). Boston, MA: Allyn & Bacon.

Mao, Y., Peng, K. Z., & Wong, C. (2012). Indigenous research on Asia: In search of the emic components of *guanxi. Asia Pacific Journal of Management, 29*(4), 1143–1168.

ACTIVITY 2.4
MEASURING ETHNICITY

Researchers of culture and psychology often include a measure of ethnicity in their studies. In everyday conversation, the terms ethnicity, race, and nationality are often used interchangeably, but there are important distinctions. Ethnicity refers to a group's shared characteristics, typically a common heritage, often with a connection to a specific geographical location. Race refers more to the physical characteristics of a person, such as skin color, although racial categories are socially constructed and differ from society to society. Nationality is another way to indicate citizenship or the nation with which one identifies. Hector Betancourt and Steven Regeser López (1993) noted that ethnicity is often a means by which cultural values and beliefs are transmitted. This activity encourages you to explore some of the ways ethnicity is measured in psychological research and to think critically about the validity of these measurement techniques.

Directions: In response to the items below, develop different measures of ethnicity. You need not actually administer these measures, but it might be helpful to think about how people with various ethnic backgrounds might respond to them.

Measurements

1. Write a free-response questionnaire item (an item that does not give any options but is open-ended) asking the respondent to simply state his or her ethnicity.

2. Write a questionnaire item that includes a checklist of ethnic categories from which the respondent chooses in order to indicate his or her ethnicity.

---

3. Write a questionnaire item that asks the respondent to report his or her ethnic ancestry in terms of a proportional representation of his or her parents' or grandparents' ethnicity (in terms of fractions or percentages).

4. For this question only, you are asked to think about how you would measure the degree to which someone identifies with a *specific* ethnic group. Write a questionnaire item that asks the respondent about behaviors (such as food, hobbies, reading material, or cultural practices) that are seen as indicative of a particular ethnicity. For example, a behavioral measure of French Canadian ethnicity might be "Do you read French language news?" Specify below the ethnicity you are assessing and write at least five behavioral items for that cultural group.

5. What are the advantages and disadvantages of the free-response measure?

6. What are the advantages and disadvantages of the checklist measure?

7. Under what circumstances might the proportional ancestry measure be useful?

8. Under what circumstances might the behavioral measure be useful?

9. Which of the four measures do you view as generally the most accurate way to assess ethnicity? The least accurate? Please explain.

10. Which type of measure best assesses *your* ethnicity? Please explain.

Thinking Further

1. Joseph Trimble (1990) coined the term "ethnic gloss" to refer to overgeneralized labels used to categorize ethnocultural groups. For example, Trimble and Bhadra (2013) noted that the single category "American Indian" is used to refer to over 500 individual tribal units, varying widely in terms of language and belief systems.

    What is another example of ethnic gloss? Why might ethnic gloss be problematic in research on culture and psychology?

2. Measuring ethnic categories is quite different from measuring the *extent* to which an individual identifies with that category (Connelly, Gayle, & Lambert, 2016). For example, the items in Jean Phinney's Multigroup Ethnic Identity Measure-Revised (MEIM-R; Phinney, 2007) are designed to measure the degree to which respondents have explored and are committed to their ethnic identity.

    In the space below, write a research question that might be addressed by data from an ethnic identity measure like the MEIM-R.

References

Connelly, R., Gayle, V., & Lambert, P. S. (2016). Ethnicity and ethnic group measures in social survey research. *Methodological Innovations*, *9*, 1–10.

Betancourt, H., & López, S. R. (1993). The study of culture, ethnicity, and race in American psychology. *American Psychologist*, *48*(6), 629–637.

Phinney, J., & Ong, A. (2007). Conceptualization and measurement of ethnic identity: Current status and future directions. *Journal of Counseling Psychology*, *54*(3), 271–281.

Trimble, J. E. (1990). Ethnic specification, validation prospects and future of drug abuse research. *International Journal of the Addictions*, *25*, 149–169.

Trimble, J. E., & Bhadra, M. (2013). Ethnic gloss. In K. Keith (Ed.), *Encyclopedia of cross-cultural psychology* (pp. 500–504). London, UK: Wiley-Blackwell.

ACTIVITY 2.5
WRITING TRANSLATABLE ITEMS

There is much controversy among those who study culture and psychology over the wisdom of translating materials developed in one culture for use in assessing the behaviors of individuals in another culture. However, most would agree that if translation is to be used, there are practices that increase its accuracy. The purpose of this activity is to explore the process of preparing test materials for translation.

Directions: Using library resources (such as PsycINFO), locate a scale or test that is designed to measure some psychological phenomenon. Two good sources to help you identify tests in your area of interest are the *Mental Measurements Yearbook*, which contains descriptions, reviews, and references for hundreds of tests, and *Tests in Print*, which is a bibliography of commercially available tests. Once you have located a scale, choose five items of interest to you and write them below. Next, modify the wording of the items based on the rules on the following page, which were adapted from Richard Brislin, Walter Lonner, and Robert Thorndike's (1973) guidelines for writing translatable items.

1. State the author, source, and name of the scale.

2. List five of the original scale items.

   a.

   b.

   c.

   d.

   e.

Guidelines for Writing Translatable Items

1. Use short, simple sentences.
2. Use active rather than passive words.
3. Repeat nouns instead of using pronouns.
4. Avoid metaphor and colloquialisms.
5. Avoid the subjunctive tense (such as verb forms with *could* or *would*).
6. Avoid adverbs and prepositions telling where or when (such as *frequent, beyond, upper*).
7. Avoid possessive forms.
8. Use specific rather than general terms (such as *cow, chicken,* or *pig* rather than *livestock*).
9. Avoid words indicating vagueness regarding some event or thing (such as *probably* or *frequently*).
10. Avoid sentences with two different verbs if the verbs indicate two different actions.

3. List the five modified items.

   a.

   b.

   c.

   d.

   e.

Source

Guidelines for writing translatable items adapted from Brislin, R., Lonner, W., & Thorndike, R. *Cross-cultural research methods.* Copyright © 1973 by John Wiley & Sons, Inc. Adapted with permission.

ACTIVITY 2.6
BACK-TRANSLATION

One of the many concerns in conducting cross-cultural research is the accuracy of translated materials. This activity will provide you with an opportunity to try out a widely used technique for improving the quality of translated materials called *back-translation* (Brislin, 1980; 2000).

Directions: For this activity you will need to enlist the help of two bilingual individuals who are skilled in the same languages. The materials to be translated are the five test items you developed in Activity 2.5 or any other five psychological test items. The first bilingual individual is to translate the test items from the original language to a second (or target) language. You are then to hand the translated version to a second bilingual individual who is to translate them back into their original language. The two bilingual assistants are to work separately on this task. By comparing the original and back-translated version of the test items you can identify concepts or word forms that cannot be accurately translated.

1. State the author, source, name of the scale, and original language.

2. What is the target language for your translation?

3. List your five items from Activity 2.5 or other source.

   a.

   b.

   c.

   d.

   e.

---

4. List the items as translated into the target language.

a.

b.

c.

d.

e.

5. List the five items as back translated into the original language.

a.

b.

c.

d.

e.

6. List below any words or phrases that did not translate accurately or were difficult to translate. What might problems in translation tell you about cultural differences?

7. Based on the results of the back-translation, are there any modifications you think would be useful to make to the *original* version to allow for a translation into equivalent versions? Please explain.

Thinking Further

Perspectives on translation have changed since back-translation was first introduced, with a greater focus on the context around the material to be translated. Sonia Colina, Nicole Marrone, Maia Ingram and Daisey Sánchez (2017) suggested that the back-translation method focuses too much on the text to be translated and recommended that translations also consider characteristics of the audience (e.g., age, socioeconomic status), the communication method (e.g., read by the participant, spoken by an interviewer) and the purpose (e.g., to gather opinions, make a diagnosis). How might these factors play a role in the translation you conducted?

References

Brislin, R. (1980). Translation and content analysis of oral and written materials. In H. Triandis & J. Berry (Eds.), *Handbook of cross-cultural psychology: Vol.2: Methodology* (pp. 389–444). Boston, MA: Allyn & Bacon.

Brislin, R. W. (2000). Back-translation. In A. E. Kazdin (Ed.), *Encyclopedia of psychology: Vol. 1*. (pp. 359–360). Washington, DC: American Psychological Association.

Colina, S., Marrone, N., Ingram, M., & Sánchez, D. (2017). Translation quality assessment in health research: A functionalist alternative to back-translation. *Evaluation & the Health Professions*, *40*(3), 267–293.

ACTIVITY 2.7
PAGTATANONG-TANONG: AN INDIGENOUS
RESEARCH METHOD

This activity evaluates the cross-cultural applicability of the research methods typically used in "Western psychology" and explores an indigenous research method from the Philippines called *pagtatanong-tanong.*

Directions: Read the scenario and answer the questions that follow.

Scenario: Suppose that you have been trained at your university to uphold the following principles of research:

- The researcher must remain objective. It is important not to become too emotionally attached, or disclose personal information, to research participants.
- Procedures should be standardized. The questions asked of participants and the conditions under which they are asked should be as uniform as possible.
- Participants should not be subject to the influence of others during the testing or interview process (unless it is a condition of the experiment). Thus, participants should be tested or interviewed on an individual basis.

Now imagine that you are preparing to conduct a series of interviews in a rural community in the Philippines. Through reading and speaking with experts and members of this community you learn the following about the culture in which you are planning to conduct your research.

- People are unaccustomed to being asked a series of questions in sequence and responding in a regimented manner.
- People are uncomfortable discussing personal opinions or behaviors with a stranger with whom there will be no future relationship.
- People are more comfortable speaking in a conversational manner in which each person discloses information and contributes to managing the process and content of the conversation.
- People may be uncomfortable alone with a stranger, particularly if the stranger is of a different gender or social status.

---

1. Describe how you might modify your research methods in order to conduct your interviews more effectively. Which research principles would you be willing to reconsider, and which principles would you maintain?

2. Rogelia Pe-Pua (1989; 2006) described a social science research method indigenous to the Philippines called *pagtatanong-tanong*. According to Pe-Pua, *pagtatanong-tanong* has some of the following characteristics:

   - The researcher uses a tentative outline of questions that are revised based on input from the participants.
   - The researcher and the participants share equally in determining the content and structure of the interview.
   - A relationship is established between the researcher and the participants such that the participants feel comfortable asking the researcher questions and expect that they may have contact with the researcher in the future.
   - The researcher starts interviewing with a group of participants. Interruptions in the interview process are not seen as distractions, but as an opportunity to check on the reliability of information obtained.

What do you expect about the validity of the information you would collect in a rural community in the Philippines using the *pagtatanong-tanong* method?

Thinking Further

If you are not from the rural Philippines yourself, do you think that *pagtatanong-tanong* would yield useful information in your culture? Please explain.

References

Pe-Pua, R. (1989). Pagtatanong-tanong: A cross-cultural research method. *International Journal of Intercultural Relations*, *13*, 147–163.

Pe-Pua, R. (2006). From decolonizing psychology to the development of a cross-indigenous perspective in methodology: The Philippine experience. In U. Kim, K.-S. Yang, & K.-K. Hwang (Eds.), *Indigenous and cultural psychology: Understanding people in context* (pp. 109–137). New York, NY: Springer.

ACTIVITY 2.8
ETHICS IN CROSS-CULTURAL RESEARCH

You are probably familiar with many of the ethical concerns faced by psychologists, such as obtaining informed consent from potential research participants, protecting them from harm and discomfort, and fully debriefing participants once the research has been completed. This activity encourages you to think about the additional ethical issues cross-cultural psychologists must address.

Directions: Read the following scenario and identify any ethical dilemmas. Next, propose an alternative research design that will remedy each ethical concern.

Scenario: A study conducted in the United States by Leanne ten Brinke, Poruz Khambatta, and Dana Carney (2015) found that people were less successful in deceiving others when telling lies in a sparse environment (an empty office) than when telling lies in an enriched environment (a decorated and furnished office). The authors reasoned that a sparse environment creates feelings of discomfort and powerlessness, which results in the leakage of cues to deception. A German researcher wonders if these findings would hold true in a natural environment as well. He decides to test this idea by replicating the study in two regions of Mexico, where he will be spending his vacation, one a desert environment (sparse) and the other a tropical environment (enriched). He reasons that since both are in the same country, this would eliminate any cultural differences between the two regions, which could be confounded with the differences in (sparse/enriched) environment. Early in the research process he befriends a local high school teacher and soon involves him in the project. The teacher takes primary responsibility for identifying potential research participants, translating data, and acting as a liaison with local authorities. The teacher also spends a considerable amount of time discussing possible interpretations of the data with the researcher. Participants are asked to sign an informed consent form prior to the start of the study and are given the researcher's email address in case any questions or concerns arise. The study, which is documented with both written and video records, identifies individuals in each location who are able to deceive others effectively. The research participants are paid the same amount of money per hour that the researcher has paid participants in Germany, though this is a large amount in terms of the local economy. Once the study is completed, the researcher returns to Germany to present his findings at a national conference, using the video materials as illustration. A few months later, he is sole author of a journal article reporting the results of this study.

1. Discuss each of the ethical concerns illustrated by the above scenario.

2. Propose an alternative research design to remedy the ethical limitations of this study.

Reference

ten Brinke, L., Khambatta, P., & Carney, D. R. (2015). Physically scarce (vs. enriched) environments decrease the ability to tell lies successfully. *Journal of Experimental Psychology: General, 144*(5), 982–992.

ACTIVITY 2.9
TOWARD A MORE INCLUSIVE PSYCHOLOGY

If psychology as a discipline is to become more inclusive, those who consume and design psychological research will need to become more aware of various forms of bias. The purpose of this activity is to familiarize you with some of the forms of bias that frequently occur in studying psychological processes.

Directions: Read the research project descriptions below and identify the form(s) of bias in each.

1. In a study of attachment behavior and academic achievement, children and their mothers are observed and interviewed at great length to determine the nature and degree of the bond between them.

2. A researcher is interested in investigating how gender roles may influence attraction in online dating. She has women rate profiles of men, and men rate profiles of women, that vary in attractiveness and conformity to traditional gender roles.

3. A researcher is interested in studying social interaction between people with and without disabilities. He simulates disability by having a nondisabled student confederate sit in a wheelchair in the coffee shop of the student center and then observes the interaction between the confederate and the (nondisabled) students who enter the room.

4. A journal specializing in gender issues in psychology devotes an entire issue to the topic of Asian and Pacific women.

5. A study of friendship patterns in adults compares results across four different age groups. The groups consist of 18 to 29-year-olds, 30 to 45-year-olds, 46 to 59-year-olds, and individuals 60 years and over.

Sources

Project descriptions are based on the following articles:

Clarke, V., Ellis, S. J., Peel, E. A., & Riggs, D. W. (2010). *Lesbian, gay, bisexual, trans and queer psychology: An introduction*. Cambridge, UK: Cambridge University Press.

Denmark, F. L. (1994). Engendering psychology. *American Psychologist, 49*, 329–334.

Fine, M., & Asch, A. (1988). Disability beyond stigma: Social interaction, discrimination, and activism. *Journal of Social Issues, 44*, 3–21.

Reid, P. T., & Kelly, K. (1994). Research on women of color: From ignorance to awareness. *Psychology of Women Quarterly, 18*, 477–486.

Schaie, K. W. (1988). Ageism in psychological research. *American Psychologist, 43*, 179–183.

ACTIVITY 2.10
DESIGNING CROSS-CULTURAL RESEARCH

Designing research that compares cultures on some psychological phenomenon involves several steps beyond what is required for research within a single culture. It rarely makes sense to conduct the study in exactly the same way using exactly the same materials in more than one culture. Although the way the research is conducted in each culture should not be the *same*, it is important that it be *equivalent.* This activity will acquaint you with some of the forms of equivalence that must be considered in conducting cross-cultural research.

Directions: For this activity you will need to locate a journal article that reports a psychological study conducted within a single culture. Try to choose a relatively straightforward study in which the independent and dependent variables, the hypothesis, and the methods used are understandable to you. Determine in which culture you would replicate the study. In practice, the choice of cultures in which to conduct research should be based on aspects of the cultures that are relevant to the theories or concepts you are testing. For this activity, however, it is more important that you choose a culture that is somewhat familiar to you. Next, answer the questions below regarding various issues of cross-cultural equivalence.

1. Provide the complete citation for the journal article you have chosen (see the reference section of activities in this book for examples of the format and content of citations).

2. Briefly describe the study that you will prepare to replicate. Include the independent and dependent variables, the hypothesis, and the methods used.

3. Describe the culture in which the above study would be replicated.

Equivalence: For each of the following forms of equivalence, determine whether the procedures used in the original study would be culturally appropriate if used in the second culture. If the procedure is not appropriate, suggest how you might modify the procedure in order to produce an outcome that is equivalent in both cultures.

1. *Conceptual equivalence.* Does the primary phenomenon being investigated have the same meaning in both cultures? For example, the concept of *parenting behavior* may not have conceptual equivalence if comparing a culture in which parents are the primary caregivers and a culture in which the extended family or siblings play a major role in childrearing.

2. *Sampling equivalence*. Does the method of recruiting research participants yield individuals who are similar on dimensions other than culture? For example, many studies are conducted with college students as participants. However, college students in a culture where a large proportion of the population attends college may differ in important ways (e.g., income, gender) from students in a culture where only the most privileged attend college.

3. *Item or task equivalence*. Do the questionnaire or interview items or experimental tasks that participants perform have the same meaning in both cultures? For example, it would be invalid for a cross-cultural study of music memory to use songs that are familiar to participants in one of the cultures and not in the other.

4. *Equivalence of the test situation*. Is the test situation likely to be perceived and valued similarly in both cultures? For example, in some cultures people are very familiar with strangers approaching them to ask somewhat personal questions as part of a study. In other cultures, this is a circumstance that would elicit suspicion and concern.

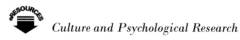

Thinking Further

Those listed above are just a few of the forms of equivalence that need to be considered when making cross-cultural comparisons. Please make suggestions below for other aspects of research design and implementation that should have equivalent meaning to participants when conducting valid cross-cultural studies.

−3−

Culture and Basic Processes

ACTIVITY 3.1
MAGICAL THINKING

Sometimes members of more traditional cultures are described as using forms of magical thinking that defy rules of logic and reason. Paul Rozin and Carol Nemeroff (2002) suggested that such thinking is not limited to traditional cultures but exists in some aspects of daily life in highly industrialized cultures as well. Their research on college students in the United States demonstrated the two forms of magical thinking below, described over a century ago by Sir James Frazer (1890/1959).

The law of contagion states that when two things (or beings) are in contact with each other the properties of one can permanently transfer to the other. For example, Frazer described an ancient Chinese practice in which burial clothes were sewn by young women with the reasoning that their longevity would somehow pass into the clothes and ensure that the clothes themselves would live long (that is, not be used for many years).

The law of similarity holds that an image of an object or person takes on the characteristics of the actual object or person. For example, Frazer noted that in many cultures it was believed that by damaging footprints it is possible to injure the person who made them.

The purpose of this activity is to explore the use of magical thinking among college students and consider the meaning of such thinking for understanding the link between culture and cognition.

Directions: Identify two college students to act as participants in this activity. Then, using the interview forms below, ask each participant the two questions about magical thinking (based on research by Rozin, Millman, & Nemeroff, 1986). Please interview the two participants separately and do not tell them that you are studying magical thinking. The first item addresses the law of contagion and the second item addresses the law of similarity.

Participant A

1. Would you rather wear a laundered shirt that had been previously worn by someone you like, someone you dislike, or someone you don't know? Please explain.

2. Would it be more difficult for you to throw darts at a dartboard depicting a picture of someone you like or someone you don't like? Please explain.

Participant B

1. Would you rather wear a laundered shirt that had been previously worn by someone you like, someone you dislike, or someone you don't know? Please explain.

2. Would it be more difficult for you to throw darts at a dartboard depicting a picture of someone you like or someone you don't like? Please explain.

To what extent did your participants manifest magical thinking (on item 1, choosing the shirt worn by the liked person, and on item 2, having more difficulty throwing darts at the liked person, indicates magical thinking)? Please explain.

Thinking Further

1. Can you think of any alternative explanations for the "magical thinking" in the two questions asked of the participants?

2. Have you engaged in any other forms of magical thinking? Please explain.

3. To what extent does magical thinking interfere with rational thinking in everyday life in your culture?

Source

Based on Rozin, P., Millman, L., & Nemeroff, C. (1986). Operation of the laws of sympathetic magic in disgust and other domains. *Journal of Personality and Social Psychology, 50,* 703–712.

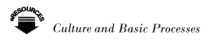

References

Frazer, J. G. (1959). *The new golden bough: A study in magic and religion.* New York: MacMillan (Edited by T. H. Gaster, 1922; Original work published 1890).

Rozin, P., Millman, L., & Nemeroff, C. (1986). Operation of the laws of sympathetic magic in disgust and other domains. *Journal of Personality and Social Psychology, 50,* 703–712.

Rozin, P., & Nemeroff, C. (2002). Sympathetic magical thinking: The contagion and similarity "heuristics." In T. Gilovich, D. Griffin, & D. Kahneman (Eds.), *Heuristics and biases: The psychology of intuitive judgment* (pp. 201–215). New York, NY: Cambridge University Press.

ACTIVITY 3.2
IMPLICIT THEORIES OF INTELLIGENCE

Patricia Ruzgis and Elena Grigorenko (1994) distinguished between cross-cultural research focusing on explicit and implicit theories of intelligence. They explained that studies of explicit theories have attempted to determine how cultural environments impact the development of different patterns of intellectual abilities. The data used to test explicit theories usually consists of scores on various tests of cognitive abilities. Explicit theories are constructed by scholars who are specialists in investigating cognitive abilities. Implicit theories, on the other hand, are the ideas that everyday people have about what constitutes intelligence. Data gathered to study implicit theories may include beliefs about the characteristics of an intelligent person or definitions of intelligence that are generated by research participants. Robert Sternberg and Elena Grigorenko (2004) have investigated implicit theories of intelligence in order to better understand cultural differences in conceptions of intelligence. In this activity, you can explore your own implicit theory of intelligence and compare it to data on implicit theories of intelligence across cultures. We will also examine the concept of *giftedness* as a way to gain further insight into beliefs about intelligence.

Directions: Please respond to each of the questions below in the space provided.

1. Describe what the term *intelligent* means to you.

2. Describe what the term *gifted* means to you.

3. Read the list of items below and put an "X" in the blank next to any characteristic you associate with *an intelligent person.*

_____ a. reasons logically

_____ b. is verbally fluent

_____ c. is sociable

_____ d. can take another's point of view

_____ e. works efficiently

_____ f. identifies connections among ideas

_____ g. speaks clearly and articulately

_____ h. is humorous

_____ i. is modest

_____ j. plans ahead

_____ k. makes clear decisions

_____ l. is knowledgeable about a particular field of study

_____ m. gets along well with others

_____ n. admits mistakes in good grace

_____ o. sees all aspects of a problem

4. For each of the items you selected above, add a point to the appropriate subscale below and calculate your scores for each of the five subscales (your scores should range from 0 to 3).

_____ Practical Problem Solving: items a., f., and o.

_____ Verbal Ability: items b., g., and l.

_____ Positive Social Competence: items c., h., and m.

_____ Receptive Social Competence: items d., i., and n.

_____ Task Efficiency: items e., j., and k.

5. Hiroshi Azuma and Keiko Kashiwagi (1987) distinguished between positive social competence and receptive social competence. Look at the items that compose each of these subscales. How would you describe the difference between these two forms of social competence?

6. Look at your scores on the Positive Social Competence and Receptive Social Competence subscales. To what extent were these subscales part of your image of an intelligent person?

7. Ruzgis and Grigorenko observed that implicit theories of intelligence in more individualistic societies tend to include forms of Positive Social Competence whereas implicit theories of intelligence in more collectivist societies tend to include forms of Receptive Social Competence. Why might Positive Social Competence be associated with individualism and Receptive Social Competence be associated with collectivism?

8. Reread your description of intelligence in question 1. Are there any characteristics in your description that would not be categorized under any of the five subscales? Please explain.

9. Carol Dweck has studied the implications of our implicit theories of intelligence for motivation to learn. She distinguished between a *fixed mindset*, the

---

belief that intelligence is a static trait that cannot be meaningfully changed, and a *growth mindset*, the belief that intelligence is a quality that can be developed through effort and the willingness to try different strategies to achieve one's goal (Dweck, 2012). Her research found that a growth mindset is associated with greater well-being and academic success. These mindsets can vary with culture. For example, Jin Li and colleagues (2014) reported that Taiwanese mothers emphasize the "learning virtues" of diligence and perseverance (consistent with a growth mindset) more than do European American mothers. Does your implicit theory include the idea that intelligence is fixed, or do you believe that it can be changed?

10. Cross-cultural researchers have observed much variability in cultural conceptions of giftedness including some cultures in which there is no term for giftedness (Sternberg, 2007). For example, Mary Romero (1994) explored the underrepresentation of American Indian children in gifted and talented programs, specifically in regard to Keresan Pueblo society. She found that the Keresan concept of giftedness reflected the collectivism of Keresan society. Giftedness required that one's unique talents or abilities contributed to the well-being of the community. Furthermore, giftedness in Keresan society did not involve distinguishing one individual over another. Reread your description of giftedness in question 2. To what extent does your description reflect individualist values? Collectivist values?

Thinking Further

Sternberg (2004, p. 326) used the term *successful intelligence* to refer to "the skills and knowledge needed for success in life, according to one's own definition of success, within one's sociocultural context." According to this definition, what skills and knowledge would be required for successful intelligence in your culture?

Sources

The Positive Social Competence, Receptive Social Competence, and Task Efficiency items were derived from Azuma, H. & Kashiwagi, K. Descriptors for an intelligent person: A Japanese Study. *Japanese Psychological Research, 29*, 17–26. Copyright © 1987 by Japanese Psychological Association. Adapted with permission.

The Practical Problem Solving and Verbal Ability items were derived from Sternberg, R. J., Conway, B. E., Ketron, J. L., & Bernstein, M. People's conceptions of intelligence. *Journal of Personality and Social Psychology, 41*, 37–55. Copyright © 1981 by American Psychological Association. Adapted with permission.

References

Azuma, H., & Kashiwagi, K. (1987). Descriptors for an intelligent person: A Japanese Study. *Japanese Psychological Research, 29*, 17–26.

Dweck, C. S. (2012). *Mindset: How you can fulfill your potential.* London: Constable & Robinson Limited.

Li, J., Fung, H., Bakeman, R., Rae, K., & Wei, W. (2014). How European American and Taiwanese mothers talk to their children about learning. *Child Development, 85*(3), 1206–1221.

Romero, M. E. (1994). Identifying giftedness among Keresan Pueblo Indians: The Keres Study. *Journal of American Indian Education, 34*, 35–58.

Ruzgis, P., & Grigorenko, E. L. (1994). Cultural meaning systems, intelligence, and personality. In R. J. Sternberg & P. Ruzgis (Eds.), *Personality and intelligence* (pp. 248–270). New York, NY: Cambridge University Press.

Sternberg, R. J. (2004). Culture and intelligence. *American Psychologist, 59*(5), 325–338.

Sternberg, R. J., & Grigorenko, E. L. (2004). Why cultural psychology is necessary and not just nice: The example of the study of intelligence. In R. J. Sternberg & E. L. Grigorenko (Eds.), *Culture and competence: Contexts of life success* (pp. 207–223). Washington, DC: American Psychological Society.

Sternberg, R. J. (2007). Cultural concepts of giftedness. *Roeper Review, 29*(3), 160–165.

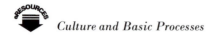
ACTIVITY 3.3
RACE AND IQ: EVALUATING THE ASSUMPTIONS

In the 1980s, it was common for psychology textbooks to mention diversity on one topic only – race and IQ. Since that time, studies attempting to find racial differences in intelligence have continued to surface from time to time, most recently due to the explosion of genetic research (Sternberg, Grigorenko, & Kidd, 2005). Many scholars have criticized the logic that forms the foundation for these studies (e.g., Colman, 2016; Nisbett, 2009). In fact, Robert Sternberg, Elena Grigorenko, and Kenneth Kidd (2005) state that race and IQ studies are based on folk beliefs rather than science. This activity explores the faulty logic of research on race and IQ.

Directions: Discuss and evaluate the logic behind one of the assumptions below. Locate and cite at least two scholarly sources (books or journal articles) to support your position.

- IQ test scores indicate fundamental intellectual ability.
- It is scientifically valid to examine "racial differences."
- Group differences in IQ reflect genetic differences.
- IQ is immutable (cannot be changed).
- High IQ leads to (causes) socioeconomic success.

Sources: In the space below, provide the full citation for your articles (see the reference section of activities in this book for examples of the format and content of citations).

Discussion:

References

Colman, A. M. (2016). Race differences in IQ: Hans Eysenck's contribution to the debate in the light of subsequent research. *Personality and Individual Differences, 103*, 182–189.

Nisbett, R. E. (2009). *Intelligence and how to get it: Why schools and cultures count.* New York: W. W. Norton & Company.

Sternberg, R. J., Grigorenko, E. L., & Kidd, K. K. (2005). Intelligence, race, and genetics. *American Psychologist, 60*, 46–59.

ACTIVITY 3.4
TESTING COGNITIVE ABILITIES ACROSS CULTURES

Cultural psychologists and cross-cultural psychologists tend to differ in their views about the usefulness of testing cognitive abilities (such as problem solving, memory, and categorization) across cultures (Greenfield, 1997). *Cross-cultural psychologists* have tended to believe that once adjustments are made to a cognitive abilities test it can be used effectively in a culture other than the one for which it was originally developed. In fact, a significant portion of cross-cultural psychology focuses on how to modify tests (such as through translation or the use of culturally familiar materials and tasks) in order to make them cross-culturally appropriate. *Cultural psychologists*, on the other hand, have tended to believe that cognitive ability tests are themselves a product of culture. Patricia Greenfield (1997) explained that *symbolic culture* – that is, shared assumptions, knowledge, and communication – is embedded in any test of cognitive ability. She argued that if the individuals tested do not share the symbolic culture of the test or tester, the result will be cultural misunderstandings that threaten the validity of the test. Greenfield recommended an alternative to taking tests from one culture and using it in another. She suggested that one should first identify cognitive abilities that are valued within a particular culture and then develop culturally appropriate ways to measure these indigenous cognitive skills. This strategy might be called an *emic*, or culture-specific, approach. The purpose of this activity is to examine how one might go about using the cultural psychologists' approach to studying cognitive abilities.

Directions: Imagine that you have been hired to develop a test of cognitive ability to be used in a culture where formal testing has never taken place.

1. Describe how you would go about determining which abilities are valued in this culture.

---

2. Describe how you would develop a measure to test those abilities.

3. Under what circumstances, if any, might it be appropriate to use a standardized cognitive abilities test (such as an IQ test) developed elsewhere in the culture described above?

Reference

Greenfield, P. M. (1997). You can't take it with you: Why ability assessments don't cross cultures. *American Psychologist, 52,* 1115–1124.

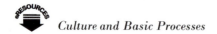

ACTIVITY 3.5
CULTURAL NEUROSCIENCE

Cultural neuroscience is a relatively new approach to studying culture and human behavior which became possible due to the mapping of the human genome and advances in brain imaging. Nicholas Rule (2014, p. 4) defined cultural neuroscience as, ". . . the application of cognitive neuroscience tools to answering questions about cultural differences in thought and behavior." A wide range of topics have been explored using this approach, including language, music, mathematics, prejudice and stereotyping, visual perception, and social cognition. This activity will acquaint you with the growing field of cultural neuroscience, some examples of which include:

- A series of studies identified a common response to infants' cries in the brains of new mothers from several different countries. Marc Bornstein and colleagues (2017) found enhanced activity in areas of the brain linked to the intention to move, speak, and caregive (the supplementary motor area, Broca's area and the superior temporal regions associated with processing speech and complex sounds, and midbrain and striatal regions associated with caregiving). This corresponds to their observations of mothers across cultures responding to their infants' cries by picking up, holding, and talking to the infant. The authors suggested that these fMRI findings indicate the presence of a universal neurobiological basis for human mothers' responses to infants' cries.
- As compared with Caucasian-Americans, Korean participants had greater activity as measured by fMRI in areas of the brain dealing with processing pain (the anterior cingulate cortex and bilateral anterior insula) when viewing scenes of others in distress (Cheon et al., 2013). The authors suggested that the ability to attend to the subjective experiences of others may be more critical in a collectivist as opposed to an individualist social context.
- Japanese, but not U.S. American, carriers of a specific variant of the 5-HTTLPR genotype associated with environmental sensitivity, showed increased attention to changes in others' facial expressions from positive to neutral (Ishii, Kim, Sasaki, Shinada, & Kusumi, 2014). One explanation is that "particular genotypes of environmental susceptibility genes predispose the carriers to respond more strongly to environmental input. Thus, when these carriers live in different cultural contexts with divergent values, expectations, and norms, they are expected to manifest those specific patterns more strongly than those who do not carry the same genotypes" (Sasaki & Kim, 2017, p. 7). The authors of this study suggested that attention to social cues of approval and disapproval, such as changes in facial expression, are more critical in the Japanese cultural context than in the U.S.

Directions: Using a psychology database such as PsycINFO, find a study that takes a conventional (non-neuroscience) approach to investigating emotions, cognition, or behavior across cultures. Then discuss how you might use a neuroscience approach to investigate this same topic.

You may need to review some of the functions of different neuroanatomical structures, genes or gene sequences in preparation for designing your study.

1. In the space below, provide the full citation for your article (see the reference section of activities in this book for examples of the format and content of citations).

2. Summarize the research question investigated in the study you selected.

3. Discuss how you would use a neuroscience approach to augment the methods used in the study you selected.

References

Bornstein, M. H., Putnick, D. L., Rigo, P., Esposito, G., Swain, J. E., Suwalsky, J. T. D., Su, X., Du, X., Zhang, K., Cote, L. R., De Pisapia, N., & Venuti, P. (2017). Neurobiology of culturally common maternal responses to infant cry. *PNAS Proceedings of the National Academy of Sciences of the United States of America*, *114*(45), E9465–E9473.

Cheon, B. K., Im, D., Harada, T., Kim, J., Mathur, V. A., Scimeca, J. M., Parrish, T. B., Park, H. W., & Chiao, J. Y. (2013). Cultural modulation of the neural correlates of emotional pain perception: The role of other-focusedness. *Neuropsychologia*, *51*(7), 1177–1186.

Ishii, K., Kim, H. S., Sasaki, J. Y., Shinada, M., & Kusumi, I. (2014). Culture modulates sensitivity to the disappearance of facial expression associated with serotonin transporter polymorphism (5-HTTLPR). *Culture and Brain*, *2*, 72–88.

Rule, N. O. (2014). Cultural neuroscience: A historical introduction and overview. *Online Readings in Psychology and Culture*, *9*(2). Retrieved from https://doi.org/10.9707/2307-0919.1128

Sasaki, J. Y., & Kim, H. S. (2017). Nature, nurture, and their interplay: A review of cultural neuroscience. *Journal of Cross-Cultural Psychology*, *48*, 4–22.

ACTIVITY 3.6
CULTURE AND MEMORY STRATEGIES

Memory researchers distinguish between the *structural features* of memory (such as the sensory register, rate of forgetting and working memory) and *control processes*, which are the intentional memory strategies used to manage the flow of information within and between the structural components (such as chunking and rehearsal). Ype Poortinga and Fons van de Vijver (2004) stated that the structural features appear to be universal across cultures whereas the control processes vary depending upon the context of the memory task. This activity demonstrates the impact of the context on control processes.

Directions: Complete each of the memory tasks below and answer the questions that follow.

1. Quickly read through the list of words below then cover the list with a sheet of paper and in the space to the right of the list, write down all the words that you remember.

   - hammer
   - envelope
   - pen
   - dish
   - ink
   - wrench
   - screwdriver
   - spoon
   - eraser
   - fork
   - pliers
   - paper

2. Describe the strategy you used to memorize the list of words.

 *Culture and Basic Processes*

3. In the space below, list the planets of the solar system.

4. Describe the strategy you used to recall the planets.

5. In the space below, draw a map of your campus.

6. Describe the strategy you used to remember the layout of your campus.

7. Based on this activity, what do you conclude about the impact of the context on control processes?

Thinking Further

1. Michael Ross and Qi Wang (2010) reported that as compared with people from East Asian cultures, those from European and North American cultures are better able to visualize and recall autobiographical memories, such as childhood events. How might this finding help us understand cultural differences in memory?

2. A series of studies (e.g., Masuda, Gonzalez, Kwan, & Nisbett, 2008; Masuda & Nisbett, 2001) found that when presented with a scene, U.S. American participants tended to focus on objects in the foreground whereas Japanese participants attended equally to both the foreground objects and the background context. This difference in analytic (context independent) versus holistic (context dependent) attention has been attributed in part to the finding that Japanese environments often include more elements and are more ambiguous than U.S. American environments. In fact, when participants from the U.S. and Japan were exposed to either a U.S. or Japanese street scene, both the Japanese and American participants who viewed the Japanese scenes attended more to contextual information than did those who viewed the American scenes (Miyamoto,

Nisbett, & Masuda, 2006). How might this finding help us understand cultural differences in memory?

3. Research on culture and memory has generally found that individuals who do not attend school perform poorly compared to schooled individuals on tasks involving memorizing lists of items, but that the two groups do equally well memorizing the items if they are placed in a diorama of a familiar setting (Cole, 2005). How might this finding help us understand cultural differences in memory?

4. Research on culture and memory has generally found that individuals from cultures with a strong oral tradition may be quite skilled in memorizing large amounts of information relevant to daily life (Wang & Ross, 2007), such as family histories, star positions for navigating by sea, or agricultural facts. How might this finding help us understand cultural differences in memory?

5. Studies have connected smartphone use with decreased ability to attend to and remember information (Wilmer, Sherman, & Chein, 2017). In fact, news stories have reported individuals who lose their phone and are unable to contact their spouse, close friends, or family because they don't know their phone numbers! How might this finding help us understand cultural differences in memory?

6. Based on this activity, what do you conclude about the impact of the culture on memory?

References

Cole, M. (2005). Cross-cultural and historical perspectives on the developmental consequences of education. *Human Development, 48*, 195–216.

Masuda, T., Gonzalez, R., Kwan, L., & Nisbett, R. E. (2008). Culture and aesthetic preference: Comparing the attention to context of East Asians and Americans. *Personality and Social Psychology Bulletin, 34*(9), 1260–1275.

Masuda, T., & Nisbett, R. E. (2001). Attending holistically vs. analytically: Comparing the context sensitivity of Japanese and Americans. *Journal of Personality and Social Psychology, 81*, 922–934.

Miyamoto, Y., Nisbett, R. E., & Masuda, T. (2006). Culture and the physical environment: Holistic versus analytic perceptual affordances. *Psychological Science, 17*(2), 113–119.

Poortinga, Y. H., & Van De Vijver, F. J. R. (2004). Culture and cognition: Performance differences and invariant structures. In R. J. Sternberg & E. L. Grigorenko (Eds.), *Culture and competence: Contexts of life success* (pp. 139–162). Washington, DC: American Psychological Society.

Ross, M., & Wang, Q. (2010). Why we remember and what we remember: Culture and autobiographical memory. *Perspectives on Psychological Science, 5*(4), 401–409.

Wang, Q., & Ross, M. (2007). Culture and memory. In S. Kitayama & D. Cohen (Eds.), *Handbook of cultural psychology* (pp. 645–667). New York, NY: Guilford Press.

Wilmer, H. H., Sherman, L. E., & Chein, J. M. (2017). Smartphones and cognition: A review of research exploring the links between mobile technology habits and cognitive functioning. *Frontiers in Psychology, 25*(8), 605.

ACTIVITY 3.7
CULTURE AND AESTHETIC PREFERENCE

A fascinating way to explore culture and perception is to examine aesthetic responses. Aesthetic responses refer to perceiving something (such as artwork, music, poetry, or architecture) as pleasant, beautiful, attractive, or rewarding as opposed to unpleasant, ugly, unattractive or unrewarding (Russell, Deregowski, & Kinnear, 1997). By observing styles of art, music, architecture, and the like across cultures, we would quickly conclude that cultures vary markedly in what is deemed aesthetically pleasing. But are there any universal aspects of aesthetics that might be uncovered through cross-cultural research?

Daniel Berlyne (1960) proposed that several characteristics of a stimulus, called *collative variables*, may operate across cultures to determine aesthetic preferences. One of these collative variables is complexity. Several cross-cultural studies have found a curvilinear relationship between complexity and aesthetic preference (that is, preference was greatest for moderate levels of complexity), although individual and cultural differences also influence the direction of this relationship. For example, Nichola Street and colleagues (2016) tested preference for fractal images at different levels of complexity among a large number of participants from locations in Europe, North America, Central Asia, and Africa. They reported that although age, gender, and culture played a significant role in aesthetic preferences, the responses as a whole supported preference for a moderate level of complexity. This activity explores the hypothesis that aesthetic preference is related to the complexity of the stimulus.

Directions: On the following pages you will find three drawings – one is relatively simple, another moderately complex, and another highly complex. Identify ten individuals to participate in this activity. Meet with each participant individually. Print out each drawing and place all three in front of your participant at once. Then ask him or her to rate the three items to indicate which they like most and like least (you might vary the order in which you place the drawings for different participants). Record the responses on the data sheet below by putting a "1" in the blank to indicate "most liked," a "3" to indicate "least liked," and a "2" to indicate the second-ranked stimulus. Once you have collected ratings of the three stimuli from each of your ten participants, calculate the average rating for each level of complexity. Then answer the questions that follow.

Data Sheet

	Level of Complexity		
Participant	Low	Moderate	High
1			
2			
3			
4			
5			
6			
7			
8			
9			
10			
Total Score			
Average Score			

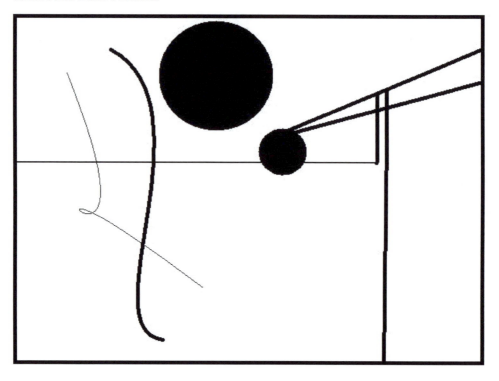

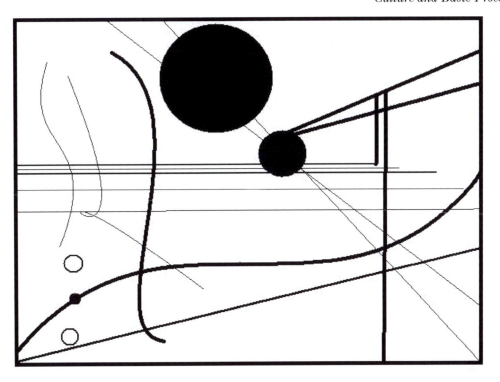

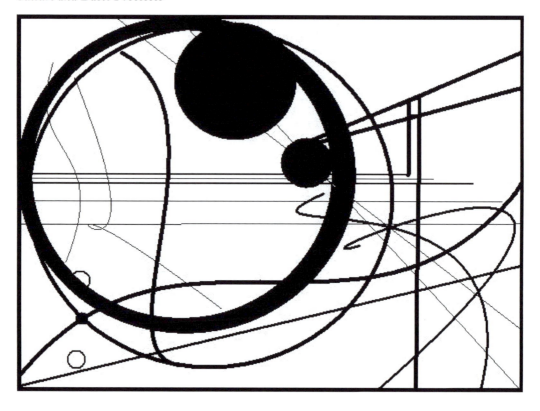

1. Did your data support a relationship between level of complexity and aesthetic preference? If so, please explain the nature of that relationship.

2. If you were to replicate this study with participants from markedly different cultures, what changes might you need to make in terms of the methods you used?

3. Alexandra Forsythe and colleagues (2008) demonstrated that familiarity influences the extent to which we perceive an object as complex, with unfamiliar images viewed as more complex. How might you build a familiarity variable into the study you conducted?

Thinking Further

This activity has focused primarily on underlying similarities in aesthetic preferences across cultures. Describe below one factor that might help explain cultural *differences* in aesthetic preferences.

Drawings: Lauren Hisada (2006)

References

Berlyne, D. E. (1960). *Conflict, arousal, and curiosity*. New York, NY: McGraw-Hill.
Forsythe, A., Mulhern, G., & Sawey, M. (2008). Confounds in pictorial sets: The role of complexity and familiarity in basic-level picture processing. *Behavior Research Methods*, *40*(1), 116–129.
Russell, P. A., Deregowski, J. B., & Kinnear, P. R. (1997). Perception and aesthetics. In J. W. Berry, P. R. Dasen, & T. S. Saraswathi (Eds.), *Handbook of cross-cultural psychology: Vol 2. Basic processes and human development* (2nd ed., pp. 107–142). Boston, MA: Allyn & Bacon.
Street, N., Forsythe, A. M., Reilly, R., Taylor, R., & Helmy, M. S. (2016). A complex story: Universal preference vs. individual differences shaping aesthetic response to fractals patterns. *Frontiers in Human Neuroscience*, *10*, 14.

ACTIVITY 3.8
INTERPLANETARY PERCEPTION

This activity explores an experiment in interplanetary perception as a way to better understand the role of culture in shaping the way we perceive stimuli.

On March 3, 1972, *Pioneer 10* was the first spacecraft to leave our solar system. It included a unique attempt to communicate with extraterrestrial life. Its message took the form of a 6- by 9-inch gold anodized plaque that had been designed by astronomer Carl Sagan. It was hoped that the message might be intercepted by intelligent inhabitants of another star system who would be able to "read" its contents. The spacecraft's signal was last detected on January 23, 2003. As William Gudykunst and Young Yun Kim (2003) observed, the *Pioneer 10* plaque illustrates the nonverbal strategy typically taken when communication involves individuals who do not share a common language. Nonverbal communication across cultures is used by many types of sojourners. This activity encourages you to think about the impact of culture on perception and the challenges of communicating nonverbally across cultures.

The components of the plaque (depicted below) are as follows:

1. The brackets indicate the height of the woman in comparison to the spacecraft. The man's arm is raised in a gesture of goodwill.
2. This figure represents a reverse in the direction of the spin of the electron in a hydrogen atom.
3. This represents the number 8 in binary form, indicating that the woman is 168 cm or 5'5" tall.
4. This radial pattern indicates the location of our solar system in the galaxy.
5. The shorter solid bars indicate directions to various pulsars from our sun and the periods of the pulsars in binary form, allowing the recipient to estimate the time the *Pioneer* was launched.
6. This indicates our solar system with the *Pioneer* originating from the Earth.

Directions: Examine the illustration of the *Pioneer 10* plaque above and read the description of its components. Then, in the space provided, draw on your knowledge of culture and perception to evaluate the likelihood that the plaque could effectively communicate with extraterrestrials. Below you will find two hints to start off your thinking on this matter.

Hint #1: A study by Wendy Winter (1963) explored the perception of safety posters by Bantu industrial workers. This study identified several instances in which the artist's symbolic meanings were not interpreted as intended, particularly when the perceiver had not attended school or was from a rural area. For example, a red star intended as an indication that someone was hit by an object was often thought to represent fire.

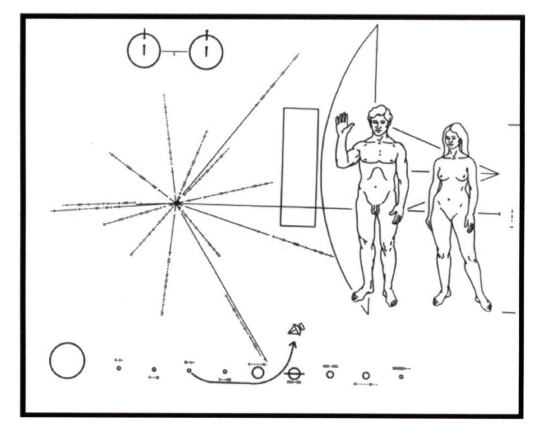

Hint #2: A significant number of cross-cultural studies have examined the perception of three-dimensional objects depicted in two dimensions (as in a photograph or drawing). These studies (e.g., Deregowski & Bentley, 1986; Hudson, 1960; McGurk & Jahoda, 1975) indicated that the ability to perceive depth in such pictures varies greatly with educational background and the nature of the task.

Discuss below the likelihood that the plaque could effectively communicate with extraterrestrials:

References

Deregowski, J. B., & Bentley, A. M. (1986). Perception of pictorial space by Bushmen. *International Journal of Psychology, 21,* 51–119.

Gudykunst, W. B., & Kim, Y. Y. (2003). *Communicating with strangers: An approach to intercultural communication* (4th ed.). New York: McGraw-Hill.

Hudson, W. (1960). Pictorial depth perception in sub-cultural groups in Africa. *Journal of Social Psychology, 52,* 183–208.

McGurk, H., & Jahoda, G. (1975). Pictorial depth perception by children in Scotland and Ghana. *Journal of Cross-Cultural Psychology, 6,* 279–296.

Winter, W. (1963). The perception of safety posters by Bantu industrial workers. *Psychologia Africana, 10,* 127–135.

ACTIVITY 3.9
SOUND SYMBOLISM

Clearly there are large differences between languages, but is there something universal about the way sounds are perceived across languages as well? This activity will familiarize you with the phenomenon of sound symbolism (once more commonly referred to as phonetic symbolism). This term refers to the idea that speech sounds may themselves carry some universal meaning, regardless of the language in which they are found. Edward Sapir's (1929) article on phonetic symbolism was one of the earliest cross-cultural research reports to be published in a psychological journal. Examples of recent research on this topic include studies of developmental changes in children's sensitivity to sound symbolism (Tzeng, Nygaard, & Namy, 2017) and the impact of sound symbolism on the ease of learning new words (Lockwood, Dingemanse, & Hagoort, 2016).

Directions: For each of the word pairs, place the letter after the word with the corresponding English meaning. For example, for the first word pair in Mandarin, if you believe *mei* means beautiful and *ch'ou* means ugly, place a (b) next to *mei* and a (u) next to *ch'ou*. If you believe *ch'ou* means beautiful and *mei* means ugly, place a (b) next to *ch'ou* and a (u) next to *mei*. Of course, if you are familiar with any of the three languages then you should not complete the word pairs for those languages.

English	**Mandarin**	**Czech**	**Hindi**
1. beautiful (b)	mei	osklivost	badsurat
ugly (u)	ch'ou	krasa	khubsurat
2. blunt (b)	k'uai	tupy	tez
sharp (s)	tun	spicaty	gothil
3. bright (b)	liang	tmavy	chamakdar
dark (d)	an	svetly	drundhala
4. fast (f)	man	rychly	tez
slow (s)	k'uai	pomaly	sust
5. hard (h)	kang	mekky	sakht
soft (s)	jou	tvrdy	narm
6. light (l)	chung	tezky	wazani
heavy (h)	ch'ing	lehky	halka
7. warm (w)	nuan	teply	thanda
cool (c)	liang	chladny	garam
8. wide (w)	chai	siroky	chaura
narrow (n)	k'uan	uzky	tang

Scoring: Check your responses against the answers at the back of this book. Circle all correct word pairs. The higher the number of correct choices, the stronger the evidence for sound symbolism (remember that by chance you would correctly identify 12 of the 24 word pairs).

Number of correct responses: ____/24

Thinking Further

What might be the source of similar sound-meaning associations across languages? How might they have developed?

Source

Adapted from Brown, R. N., Black, A. H., & Horowitz, A. E. (1955). Phonetic symbolism in natural languages. *Journal of Abnormal and Social Psychology, 50*(3), 388–393.

References

Lockwood, G., Dingemanse, M., & Hagoort, P. (2016). Sound-symbolism boosts novel word learning. *Journal of Experimental Psychology: Learning, Memory, and Cognition, 42*(8), 1274–1281.

Sapir, E. (1929). A study in phonetic symbolism. *Journal of Experimental Psychology, 12*, 225–239.

Tzeng, C. Y., Nygaard, L. C., & Namy, L. L. (2017). Developmental change in children's sensitivity to sound symbolism. *Journal of Experimental Child Psychology, 160*, 107–118.

ACTIVITY 3.10
LINGUISTIC RELATIVITY

One of the earliest topics of cross-cultural research was the relationship between language and thought. Benjamin Whorf (1956) proposed that the structure of the language one speaks influences how one views the world. This concept has been called *linguistic relativity*. For example, Jamake Highwater (1981) suggested that English speakers and speakers of the Blackfeet Indian language see the world differently. He described how he was appalled to learn that English speakers use the word *wilderness* to describe the forest. From Highwater's Blackfeet Indian perspective, it is the cities that are wild and need taming rather than the forest, which is the natural state of the world.

A stronger version of this "Whorfian hypothesis" (also called the "Sapir-Whorf hypothesis" due to assistance Whorf received from linguist Edward Sapir) is that the language we speak *determines* the kinds of thoughts and perceptions we are capable of having. This idea is known as *linguistic determinism*. Many decades of linguistic, psychological, and anthropological research have provided conditional support for linguistic relativity in certain contexts (such as spatial and numerical tasks). There has been less enthusiasm for the concept of linguistic determinism.

For example, you may be familiar with the Chihuahua dog breed, but did you know that there are "deer head" and "apple head" varieties? After learning these terms, do you think you would more easily recognize the two types of Chihuahua (linguistic relativity)? Do you think you would be unable to differentiate between types if you did not know these terms (linguistic determinism)? This activity explores the concepts of linguistic relativity and linguistic determinism and asks you to consider the validity of the Whorfian hypothesis.

Directions: This activity requires that you collect three terms used by a subculture of interest to you. For example, Jerry Dunn (1997) investigated the specialized terms used by 75 subcultural groups, including mountain bike riders, disc jockeys, tabloid reporters, frisbee players, funeral directors, surfers, FBI agents, and science fiction fans. You can find such terms by interviewing group members, exploring their websites, or reading the literature of a particular subculture. Once you have collected the three terms, respond to the questions below. The terms should refer *to concepts that are new to you.* It is important that you do not use new words for familiar concepts.

1. Describe the subculture that you investigated.

2. List the three subcultural terms and their definitions.

   a.

   b.

   c.

3. How might having these new terms *influence* your thoughts or perceptions (linguistic relativity)? For example, might it be easier now to recognize or to remember the concepts represented by these terms?

4. Do you think you would be unable to think about these concepts if you didn't know these terms (linguistic determinism)? Please explain.

5. What do you conclude about linguistic relativity and linguistic determinism?

Thinking Further

1. Several studies indicate that when given personality tests in two different languages bilingual people often produce two very different personality profiles (e.g., Veltkamp, Recio, Jacobs, & Conrad, 2013). Based on your knowledge of linguistic relativity, why do you think this might occur?

2. John Lucy (2016) suggested that future research might investigate the effect of increasingly standardized language (due to higher literacy rates and greater access to formal education) on thought. Based on your knowledge of linguistic relativity, what do you predict about the effect of language standardization on the diversity of cultural worldviews?

References

Dunn, J. (1997). *Idiom savant: Slang as it is slung.* New York, NY: Henry Holt.

Highwater, J. (1981). *The primal mind: Vision and reality in Indian America.* New York, NY: HarperCollins.

Lucy, J. A. (2016). Recent advances in the study of linguistic relativity in historical context: A critical assessment. *Language Learning, 66*(3), 487–515.

Veltkamp, G. M., Recio, G., Jacobs, A. M., & Conrad, M. (2013). Is personality modulated by language? *International Journal of Bilingualism, 17*(4), 496–504.

Whorf, B. L. (1956). The relation of habitual thought and behavior to language. In J. B. Carroll (Ed.), *Language, thought, and reality: Selected writings of Benjamin Lee Whorf* (pp. 134–159). Cambridge, MA: MIT Press.

–4–

Culture and Developmental Processes

ACTIVITY 4.1
PARENTAL ETHNOTHEORIES

Anthropologist Sara Harkness and psychologist Charles Super (1996; 2006) have written extensively on parents' cultural beliefs systems or what they termed *parental ethnotheories*. Jacqueline Goodnow (1996) pointed out that there are several reasons why it is useful to study parents' cultural beliefs. These beliefs (1) provide insight into the cognition and development of adults, (2) help us understand parenting behavior, (3) are one aspect of the context in which children develop, and (4) when studied across generations, can provide clues about cultural transmission and change. This activity will allow you to explore a variety of parental ethnotheories and examine the cultural basis for your own beliefs about childrearing.

Directions: Circle the number to indicate your view on each of the parental ethnotheories below.

1. Everyone in the household has responsibility for keeping an eye on a crawling child or toddler.

STRONGLY DISAGREE							STRONGLY AGREE	
1	2	3	4	5	6	7	8	9

2. Praising a child for accomplishing a task leads to disobedience and selfishness.

STRONGLY DISAGREE							STRONGLY AGREE	
1	2	3	4	5	6	7	8	9

3. It is cruel and neglectful to put a baby alone in a room to sleep.

STRONGLY DISAGREE							STRONGLY AGREE	
1	2	3	4	5	6	7	8	9

4. Massage is a critical aspect of routine care for infants.

STRONGLY DISAGREE								STRONGLY AGREE
1	2	3	4	5	6	7	8	9

5. Parents need to train their children in specific skills to prepare them for starting school.

STRONGLY DISAGREE								STRONGLY AGREE
1	2	3	4	5	6	7	8	9

6. Babies should be encouraged to "sleep through the night" as soon as possible.

STRONGLY DISAGREE								STRONGLY AGREE
1	2	3	4	5	6	7	8	9

7. Lactating women should freely nurse each other's children.

STRONGLY DISAGREE								STRONGLY AGREE
1	2	3	4	5	6	7	8	9

8. Parents should respond immediately when their infant begins to cry.

STRONGLY DISAGREE								STRONGLY AGREE
1	2	3	4	5	6	7	8	9

9. The role of parents is to protect and nurture their children, rather than stimulate their intellect.

	STRONGLY DISAGREE							STRONGLY AGREE	
	1	2	3	4	5	6	7	8	9

10. Children are happiest and most well behaved when parents keep to a set daily routine.

	STRONGLY DISAGREE							STRONGLY AGREE	
	1	2	3	4	5	6	7	8	9

11. By age six or seven, children are capable of caring for younger siblings.

	STRONGLY DISAGREE							STRONGLY AGREE	
	1	2	3	4	5	6	7	8	9

12. Parents having difficulty with childrearing should consult medical or psychological experts or books written by such experts.

	STRONGLY DISAGREE							STRONGLY AGREE	
	1	2	3	4	5	6	7	8	9

Thinking Further

1. With which parental ethnotheories did you most strongly agree? Why?

2. With which parental ethnotheories did you most strongly disagree? Why?

3. Meredith Small (1998) employed an *eco-cultural* perspective (Berry, 1976) in her approach to understanding childrearing. She described the many ways in which parenting beliefs and practices evolved in response to environmental as well as sociocultural demands. For example, she cited the case of the Ache of Paraguay who carry their children, rather than allowing them to crawl or walk – first in slings, then in baskets, and then piggyback – until they are five years old. This practice makes sense considering the hazards for a small child crawling or walking in the forest environment of the Ache. How have the parental ethnotheories of your culture evolved in response to the physical or sociocultural environment? Please give an example below.

References

Berry, J. W. (1976). *Human ecology and cognitive style: Comparative studies in cultural and psychological adaptation*. New York, NY: Sage/Halsted.

Goodnow, J. J. (1996). From household practices to parents' ideas about work and interpersonal relationships. In S. Harkness & C. M. Super (Eds.), *Parents' cultural belief systems: Their origins, expressions, and consequences* (pp. 313–344). New York, NY: Guilford.

Harkness, S., & Super, C. M. (1996). *Parents' cultural belief systems: Their origins, expressions, and consequences*. New York, NY: Guilford.

Harkness, S., & Super, C. M (2006). Themes and variations: Parental ethnotheories in Western cultures. In K. R. Rubin & O. B. Chung (Eds.), *Parenting beliefs, behaviors, and parent-child relations: A cross-cultural perspective* (pp. 61–79). New York, NY: Taylor & Francis.

Small, M. F. (1998). *Our babies, ourselves: How biology and culture shape the way we parent*. New York, NY: Anchor Books.

ACTIVITY 4.2
DEVELOPMENTAL NICHE

Sara Harkness and Charles Super created the developmental niche framework to better explain the role of culture in shaping human development. They asked, "How is it that growing up in a particular cultural setting – whether it be Boston, Rio de Janeiro, or the Serengeti plains of Tanzania – leads to the establishment of ways of thinking and acting so integral to one's identity that they will survive even radical changes of environment in later years?" (Super & Harkness, 1994, p. 95). The developmental niche is formed by three components (described below), which interact with each other and the larger environment. Although first introduced in the 1980s, this model continues to be the basis for empirical studies conducted throughout the world (Worthman, 2010). The purpose of this activity is to familiarize you with the concept of developmental niche and its role in the study of culture and human development.

Directions: For each of the three components of the developmental niche detailed below, describe your own experiences and then answer the questions that follow.

1. The physical and social setting (the child's living space, family composition, physical objects).

2. Customs and practices of child rearing (e.g., sleeping and feeding routines, childcare arrangements, interpersonal interaction styles, teaching approaches).

3. Caretaker psychology (psychological attributes of parents/caregivers and ethnotheories about the development and needs of children).

Thinking Further

1. The components of the developmental niche not only shape the child, but the child has an influence on those components. Consider your individual traits and characteristics. How might you have influenced the components of your developmental niche?

2. One's developmental niche is also influenced by the larger ecological, economic, and sociopolitical context. How have these factors influenced your own developmental niche?

3. Researchers of culture and human behavior assume that although each child's developmental niche is unique, those of children within a specific community will share common features. What aspects of your developmental niche might you have shared with others in your community?

4. Researchers have used a variety of methods to study the developmental niche. More visible aspects might be observed, whereas other aspects could only be studied through the self-reports of parents and family members through interviews, questionnaires, or diaries. What type of research methods might be most successful in obtaining information about your own developmental niche?

5. According to Adriana Molitor (2013), the components of the developmental niche work together as a system to provide children with a consistent message about the expectations of their culture. For example, Mieko Hobara (2003) studied the prevalence of transitional objects, such as stuffed animals or blankets, in young children in Japan and the United States. She found that, as compared with the children in the United States, children in Japan were less likely to have an attachment to a transitional object [setting] and were more likely to co-sleep with parents [customs and practices]. Hobara explains that in the United States parents are more likely to believe that infants need to be socialized to become independent, whereas some level of dependence or interdependence between parents and children is viewed as natural in Japan [caretaker psychology].

Consider the three components of your developmental niche. What messages did they convey to you about the expectations of your culture?

References

Hobara, M. (2003). Prevalence of transitional objects in young children in Tokyo and New York. *Infant Mental Health Journal, 24,* 174–191.

Molitor, A. (2013). Developmental niche. In K. Keith (Ed.), *Encyclopedia of cross-cultural psychology* (pp. 393–395). London, UK: Wiley-Blackwell.

Super, C. M., & Harkness, S. (1994). The developmental niche. In W. Lonner & R. Malpass (Eds.), *Psychology and culture* (pp. 95–99). Boston, MA: Allyn & Bacon.

Worthman, C. M. (2010). The ecology of human development: Evolving models for cultural psychology. *Journal of Cross-Cultural Psychology, 41*(4), 546–562.

ACTIVITY 4.3
YOUR SOCIAL NETWORKS

Across cultures, children deal with a variety of stressors. Common to children in many societies are stressors stemming from their relationships with friends and family, as well as from their academic and household responsibilities. Other stressors are more culture-specific or region-based, such as natural disasters, disease, racism, exposure to violence, economic crises, family emigration, sex discrimination, and forced marriages (Borja, Nastasi, Adelson, & Siddiqui, 2016). Research on child development across cultures increasingly indicates that the availability of social support is closely linked to a child's emotional and social well-being (Nastasi & Borja, 2016). Children's support networks help them cope with stress and develop the skills they will need to be a competent adult within their own culture. This activity will explore your own childhood support network and the competencies that developed as a result.

Directions: First think about your childhood social support network and make additions to the *types of social support* listed in the column on the left. Next, indicate with an "X" on the chart the source(s) of each type of social support listed. Finally, answer the questions that follow to examine the competencies that resulted from your social network.

	Sources of Social Support				
Types of Social Support	*Parents*	*Siblings*	*Extended Family*	*Nonfamily Adults*	*Nonfamily Children*
Play					
Emotional Support/ Comfort					
Material Goods/ Services					
Positive Feedback/ Affection					
Advice/ Information					
Other:					
Other:					

Thinking Further

1. For which types of social support were sources most available to you?

2. For which types of social support were sources least available to you?

3. Adults tend to play a reduced role in children's social support over time, particularly in more individualist societies (Borja, Nastasi, Adelson, & Siddiqui, 2016). Did the roles of peers and adults in your social support network change over time? Please explain.

4. Were there different roles for the females and males in your social support network? Did they provide social support in different ways? Please explain.

5. Has your social support system tended to encourage your independence from your family or interdependence with your family? Please explain.

6. Zoya Gubernskaya and Judith Treas (2016) found a link between the availability of mobile phones and social support received by adult children from their mothers in the 24 countries they investigated. What role does technology play currently in your access to social support?

7. Anne Marie Tietjen (1989) compared the social network of an eight-year-old Swedish girl with that of a Maisin agemate in Papua New Guinea. She suggested that the Swedish child, who interacts with a variety of caregivers and teachers in addition to her nuclear family, gains competence in establishing relationships with previously unfamiliar people. The Maisin girl, who is in daily contact with her extended family, develops skills in maintaining long-term sources of support among kin. Over time, have you learned more about how to establish new sources of social support or how to maintain existing sources of social support? Please explain.

8. What do you conclude about the types of social support available to you as a child and the competencies you developed as a result?

References

Borja, A. P., Nastasi, B. K., Adelson, E., & Siddiqui, Z. J. (2016). Cross-cultural patterns of children's phenomenology about stressors and supports. In B. K. Nastasi & A. P. Borja (Eds.), *International handbook of psychological well-being in children and adolescents* (pp. 291–309). New York, NY: Springer.

Gubernskaya, Z., & Treas, J. (2016). Call home? Mobile phones and contacts with mother in 24 countries. *Journal of Marriage and Family, 78*(5), 1237–1249.

Nastasi, B. K., & Borja, A. P. (2016). The Promoting Psychological Well-being Globally Project: Approach to data collection and analysis. In B. K. Nastasi & A. P. Borja (Eds.), *International handbook of psychological well-being in children and adolescents* (pp. 13–31). New York, NY: Springer.

Tietjen, A M. (1989). The ecology of children's social support networks. In D. Belle (Ed.), *Children's social networks and social supports* (pp. 37–69). New York, NY: Wiley.

ACTIVITY 4.4
FORMAL AND INFORMAL LEARNING

In 2015, the members of the United Nations Educational, Scientific and Cultural Organization (UNESCO) published a document in which they advocated for recognizing and valuing knowledge gained outside of a formal school environment through *informal learning*, which occurs in the course of daily life activities related to work, family or leisure (they also recognize *nonformal learning*, such as apprenticeships). For example, weaving or small-scale farming skills might be more frequently learned informally whereas mathematical skills and historical dates may be more frequently learned through formal schooling. According to UNESCO, recognizing and certifying skills learned outside of a formal school environment can lead to social and economic benefits for individuals who have not had access to an educational system or cannot provide evidence of formal education due to migration from their home country. The purpose of this activity is to explore the value of informal education and some of the ways it differs from formal schooling.

Directions: List five skills that you learned through formal education and five skills that you learned through informal means. Then answer the questions that follow to compare these two forms of learning.

Formal Education

1.

2.

3.

4.

5.

Informal Education

1.

2.

3.

4.

5.

1. For each of the following statements, indicate by marking the appropriate blank with an "X" whether it better describes formal or informal education.

	Formal	Informal
a. Learning occurs in a specified setting and time period.	_____	_____
b. Learning occurs through observation.	_____	_____
c. Emotions are kept separate from the subject matter.	_____	_____
d. The teacher has a personal connection with the subject matter.	_____	_____
e. Teachers of a specific subject are basically interchangeable.	_____	_____
f. Cooperation more than competition characterizes the interaction among learners.	_____	_____
g. The subject matter is closely tied to life experiences.	_____	_____
h. The learning process is fairly structured and predictable.	_____	_____

2. What are your thoughts about the value of the skills and knowledge you learned through informal education as compared with those you learned through formal education?

Thinking Further

1. What difficulties might arise for someone from a culture that depends heavily on informal education if they were to enter a formal schooling situation?

2. What characteristics of informal learning might be helpful to integrate into a formal educational setting?

3. Robert Serpell and Giyoo Hatano (1997) described how reading skills can be acquired outside of a school setting. What other skills that are typically taught in school might also be learned through informal means?

References

Serpell, R., & Hatano, G. (1997). Education, schooling, and literacy. In J. W. Berry, P. R. Dasen, & S. Saraswathi (Eds.), *Handbook of cross-cultural psychology: Vol. 2. Basic processes and human development* (2nd ed., pp. 339–376). Boston, MA: Allyn & Bacon.

UNESCO Institute for Lifelong Learning. (2015). *Recognition, validation and accreditation of non-formal and informal learning in UNESCO member states.* Hamburg, Germany: UNESCO.

ACTIVITY 4.5
HOME CULTURE AND SCHOOL CULTURE FIT

Cigdem Kagitcibasi (1990, 1997) stressed the importance of a fit between home culture and school environment for the academic success and well-being of children. According to Carrie Rothstein-Fisch and Elise Trumbull (2008), it is critical to structure classrooms and curricula such that they avoid putting the students' home culture in conflict with their school culture. They further suggested that

> teachers who are knowledgeable about the culture of school and culture of their students can serve as 'cultural brokers,' helping their students and students' families negotiate new cultural terrain and become biculturally proficient. . . .They can also share their cultural knowledge about families with other school personnel and help to influence the development of policies that are more culturally congruent.

> (p. xvii)

Here are some examples of interventions aimed at creating a better fit between students' home culture and school culture:

- The Alaska Native Knowledge Network (ANKN; 2017) has developed an extensive curriculum aimed adapting indigenous and Western knowledge systems to classrooms with a primarily Alaska Native student population. These resources include a focus on, for example, genealogy and oral history, the role of elders in children's education, and the importance of traditional ecological knowledge in contemporary society.
- The Center for Research on Education, Diversity, and Excellence (CREDE) Hawai'i Project (CREDE; n.d.) provides training and resources for teachers of native Hawaiian and other culturally and linguistically diverse students. Their "place-based" approach uses the local community and environment as a starting point to teach subjects across the curriculum, with themes such as gardening, the ocean, and Native Hawaiian plants.
- Carrie Rothstein-Fisch and Elise Trumbull (2008) collaborated with colleagues Patricia Greenfield and Blanca Quiroz to create The Bridging Cultures Project. This project was a five-year action research study of elementary classrooms in the U.S. with a high percentage of immigrant children from home cultures that emphasize collectivist values. These authors implemented a strategy for modifying individualist classroom structures to better fit a more collectivistic home culture, which they believe characterizes much of the world's population, including many of the Latina/o immigrant students in U.S. classrooms. For example, they emphasized group-oriented, interdependent activities, which they have found to support academic and behavioral success.

This activity will encourage you to identify cultural values in the classroom and to consider your own experience with the compatibility of home and school cultures.

Directions: After obtaining any necessary permission, observe a preschool or elementary school class in your community. Make careful notes on what you observe about the students' behavior, the teacher's behavior, and the classroom setting. Finally, write an analysis of the cultural values implicitly or explicitly expressed in the class session. For example, Rothstein-Fisch and Trumbull (2008) noted the individualist values that underlie the practice of asking students to take a vote to resolve a disagreement about choosing a class activity. They suggested that for students with a more collectivistic social orientation, this practice could actually make the conflict worse.

Classroom Description and Analysis

Thinking Further

1. Select one of the behaviors you detailed in your classroom observation notes and discuss how it might be altered to be more culturally inclusive. Be sure to avoid the use of cultural stereotypes.

2. Consider the challenges of creating a home-culture and school-culture fit with a diverse student body. For example, Manuela Lavelli, Paula Döge, and Mara Bighin (2016) described a multicultural Italian preschool setting in which the families of Romanian, Moroccan, Nigerian, and Sri Lankan immigrant children had educational goals that differed significantly from each other and from those of the teachers. These authors suggested that this could be addressed by greater cultural sensitivity in the curriculum as well as programs to create dialogue between teachers and immigrant parents. What strategies can you suggest to enhance home-culture and school-culture fit in a multicultural classroom?

3. Dina Birman and Nellie Tran (2015) described perhaps the most extreme form of home–school culture incompatibility, in which students with no experience

in formal schooling are placed in a traditional education system. How might you attempt to create a harmonious home-culture and school-culture fit in that circumstance?

4. Think about the fit between your own home culture and the school environment where your education took place. To what extent were they compatible? What changes could have been made to your classroom to make it more compatible with your home-culture?

References

Alaska Native Knowledge Network. (2017, November 27). Retrieved from https://uaf.edu/ankn/

Birman, D., & Tran, N. (2015). *The academic engagement of newly arriving Somali Bantu students in a U.S. elementary school*. Washington, DC: Migration Policy Institute.

Center for Research on Education, Diversity, and Excellence Hawai'i Project (CREDE; n.d.). Retrieved from http://manoa.hawaii.edu/coe/crede/

Kagitcibasi, C. (1990). Family and home-based intervention. In R. Brislin (Ed.), *Applied cross-cultural psychology* (pp. 121–141). Newbury Park, CA: Sage.

Kagitcibasi, C. (1997). Individualism and collectivism. In J. Berry, M. Segall, & C. Kagitcibasi (Eds.), *Handbook of cross-cultural psychology, Vol. 3: Behavior and applications* (2nd ed., pp. 1–49). Boston, MA: Allyn & Bacon.

Lavelli, M., Döge, P., & Bighin, M. (2016). Socialization goals of immigrant mothers from diverse cultures and of their children's preschool teachers in Italy. *Journal of Cross-Cultural Psychology, 47*(2), 197–214.

Rothstein-Fisch, C., & Trumbull, E. (2008). *Managing diverse classrooms: How to build on students' cultural strengths.* Alexandria, VA: Association for Supervision and Curriculum Development.

ACTIVITY 4.6
A CULTURALLY APPROPRIATE PIAGETIAN TASK

Early cross-cultural studies of cognitive abilities often found deficiencies in the mental abilities of individuals from less industrialized societies. Later studies of this type demonstrated, however, that these individuals' *performance* on cognitive tasks did not likely indicate their level of *competence*. One of the reasons for this was that the earlier studies tended to use materials that were not familiar to the participants. In a classic study demonstrating the importance of the familiarity of task materials (Irwin, Schafer, & Feiden, 1974), nonliterate Liberian adults and U.S. college students were asked to perform two sorting tasks. One task involved sorting geometric figures differing in color, shape, and number. The second task involved sorting bowls of rice that differed in size of bowl, type of rice, and cleanness of the grains. The Americans performed better than the Liberians on the geometric figures task, whereas the Liberians performed better than the Americans on the rice sorting task. Each group performed better on the task that utilized familiar materials.

A large number of cross-cultural studies of cognitive development have focused on Piagetian tasks. Jean Piaget's theory of cognitive development specifies a distinct structure of thought that differs at each of four stages of development. Cross-cultural research supports the sequence of stages described by Piaget, although the ages at which different stages are attained varies across cultures (Berry, Poortinga, Segall, & Dasen, 2002). In addition, Piaget's fourth stage of development, formal operations, may be dependent on exposure to formal schooling (Keller, 2011). Children performing tasks with familiar materials were also more likely than those using unfamiliar materials to demonstrate mastery of the stages assessed (Price-Williams, 1981). The purpose of this activity is to think about how one might develop a culturally appropriate Piagetian task.

Directions: Use an introductory or developmental psychology textbook to review the concept of Piagetian conservation. Then devise a task to test conservation of quantity, mass, or number. This task should be appropriate for children in a specific culture with which you are familiar. Use materials for this task that are commonly found in the culture you selected. For example, Geoffrey Saxe and Thomas Moylan (1982) developed a Piagetian conservation task appropriate for the Oksapmin of Papua New Guinea. The task involved the measurement of string bags, a commonly used object in Oksapmin culture and required that people understand that the length of bags remains constant regardless of whether it is measured along the arm of a child or the arm of an adult.

In the spaces provided below, indicate the culture and conservation task you have selected and then describe the task and materials used.

   1. The task below is intended to measure conservation of _____ for members of the _____ culture.

   2. Description of the task and materials:

References

Berry, J. W., Poortinga, Y. H., Segall, M. H., & Dasen, P. R. (2002). *Cross-cultural psychology: Research and applications*. Cambridge, UK: Cambridge University Press.

Irwin, M. H., Schafer, G. N., & Feiden, C. P. (1974). Emic and unfamiliar category sorting of Mano farmers and U.S. undergraduates. *Journal of Cross-Cultural Psychology, 5*, 407–423.

Keller, H. (2011). Culture and cognition: Developmental perspectives. *Journal of Cognitive Education and Psychology, 10*(1), 3–8.

Price-Williams, D. (1981). Concrete and formal operations. In R. H. Munroe, R. L. Monroe, & B. D. Whiting (Eds.), *Handbook of cross-cultural human development* (pp. 403–422). New York, NY: Garland Press.

Saxe, G. B., & Moylan, T. (1982). The development of measurement operations among the Oksapmin of Papua New Guinea. *Child Development, 53,* 1242–1248.

ACTIVITY 4.7
THE RESILIENCE OF CHILD SOLDIERS

Sadly, millions of children and adolescents throughout the world face the challenge of surviving natural and human-made disasters. These catastrophic events include tsunamis and hurricanes, war and terrorist attacks, gang violence and school shootings. In addition, although the Geneva Conventions prohibit the use of children under age 15 as soldiers, the United Nations (2016) estimated that tens of thousands of children around the world have been recruited or forced into armed groups. Research indicates that children and adolescents in these circumstances are susceptible to developmental delays, physical illness, family conflict, depression and other symptoms of post-traumatic stress (Slone & Mann, 2016). Yet, some studies point to the remarkable resilience of these children and adolescents in that many continue to thrive despite these conditions (Ungar, Lee, Callaghan, & Boothroyd, 2005). This activity will encourage you to think about the qualities of resilience that may help to protect children in disaster situations.

Directions: Read the descriptions of resilient youth below and then answer the questions that follow about children and adolescents who become soldiers.

Michael Ungar and colleagues' International Resilience Project has conducted research with at-risk children on five continents to identify the conditions that enable young people to cope with disaster. They identified seven tensions that young people must negotiate in order to thrive despite their environments (Ungar, 2006, p.57):

1. Access to material resources – Availability of financial, educational, medical and employment assistance and/or opportunities, as well as access to food, clothing, and shelter.
2. Relationships – Relationships with significant others, peers, and adults within one's family and community.
3. Identity – Personal and collective sense of purpose, self-appraisal of strengths and weaknesses, aspirations, beliefs and values, including spiritual and religious identification.
4. Power and control – Experiences of caring for oneself and others; the ability to effect change in one's social and physical environment in order to access health resources.
5. Cultural adherence – Adherence to one's local and/or global cultural practices, values, and beliefs.
6. Social justice – Experiences related to finding a meaningful role in community and social equality.

7. Cohesion – Balancing one's personal interests with a sense of responsibility to the greater good; feeling a part of something larger than oneself socially and spiritually.

Elena Grigorenko and Paul O'Keefe (2004) identified child soldiers as an extraordinary example of resilience in that they often develop skills that enable them to cope with an extremely hostile environment. These authors described the behaviors and attributes required of child soldiers as follows:

- running errands
- acting as spies and informants
- handling and caring for weapons
- handling wounds and personal needs
- understanding the hierarchy of the army
- reading and interpreting maps
- identifying with the army and seeking revenge on the enemy
- having self-pride, unit pride, and patriotism

Based on the seven tensions attained by resilient children, discuss why child soldiers might develop resilience.

Thinking Further

In what type of disaster might you expect children to be the most resilient? The least resilient? Please explain.

References

Grigorenko, E. L., & O'Keefe, P. A. (2004). What do children do when they cannot go to school? In R. J. Sternberg, & E. L. Grigorenko (Eds.), *Culture and competence: Contexts of life success* (pp. 23–53). Washington, DC: American Psychological Society.

Ungar, M. (2006). Nurturing hidden resilience in at-risk youth in different cultures. *Journal of the Canadian Academy of Child and Adolescent Psychiatry, 15*, 53–58.

Ungar, M., Lee, A. W., Callaghan, T., & Boothroyd, R. A. (2005). An international collaboration to study resilience in adolescents across cultures. *Journal of Social Work Research and Evaluation, 6*, 5–23.

United Nations. (February 12, 2016). International day against the use of child soldiers: Child soldiers are boys and girls we failed to protect. Retrieved from https://childrenandarmedconflict.un.org/press-release/international-day-against-child-soldiers-2016/

Slone, M., & Mann, S. (2016). Effects of war, terrorism and armed conflict on young children: A systematic review. *Child Psychiatry and Human Development, 47*(6), 950–965.

ACTIVITY 4.8
CULTURE AND PERCEPTIONS OF GROWING OLD

With the world's population rapidly aging, our perceptions of old age become increasingly important. Deborah Best and John Williams (1996) noted that stereotypes of elders are unlike other stereotypes in that they involve perceptions of a group of which we all expect to be a member. These authors conducted a study of young adults' views of growing old in 19 different countries on six continents: Africa (South Africa, Zimbabwe), Asia (India, Korea, Malaysia, Pakistan, Turkey), Europe (Finland, Germany, Norway, Poland, Portugal, Wales), North America (Canada, the U.S.), Oceania (New Zealand), and South America (Chile, Peru, Venezuela). The purpose of this activity is to assess your own views of growing old, compare them to the cross-cultural data reported by Best and Williams, and consider the factors that influence perceptions of elders.

Directions: Please respond to the questions below.

Attitudes Toward Aging

1. When you hear someone described as being "old," what age do you think of? At least _____ years of age.

2. When you hear someone described as being "middle aged," what age do you think of? At least _____ years of age.

3. Put an "X" next to the decade that you expect to be the most satisfying and productive years of your life.

   _____ 0–9 years   _____ 40–49 years   _____ 70–79 years

   _____ 10–19 years   _____ 50–59 years   _____ 80–89 years

   _____ 20–29 years   _____ 60–69 years   _____ 90–99 years

   _____ 30–39 years

4. Overall, how do you feel about growing older (circle the number below that indicates your answer).

   | Very Negatively | 1 | 2 | 3 | 4 | 5 | 6 | Very Positively |

Thinking Further

In answering the questions below, compare your answer to the Attitudes Toward Aging items with Best and Williams' findings.

1. On the average across the 19 countries, "old" was described by males as being at least 60 years and by females as being at least 62 years of age. Malaysian females gave the lowest minimum age for being old (53.9 years) and Portuguese females gave the highest minimum age for being old (67.9 years). Considering these results and your own response, what factors do you think contribute to one's view of the age one becomes "old"?

2. On the average across the 19 countries, "middle aged" was described by males as being at least 39 years and by females as being at least 41 years of age. Malaysian males gave the lowest minimum age for being middle aged (35.1 years) and Portuguese females gave the highest minimum age for being middle aged (47.8 years). Considering these results and your own response, what factors do you think contribute to one's view of the age one becomes "middle aged"?

3. Across the 19 countries both males and females thought their 20s and 30s would be the most satisfying and productive time of their lives. Women in more developed countries indicated somewhat later ages as being the best time in their lives. Considering these results and your own response, what factors do you think contribute to one's expectancies about the period of life that will be most satisfying or productive?

---

4. A common belief is that older people are regarded with greater respect in Eastern societies (e.g., East Asian and Southeast Asian countries) than in Western societies (e.g., Western Europe, Australia, Canada, and the United States), perhaps due to a more collectivist orientation or Confucian traditions of reverence for elders in the East. However, a meta-analysis of studies from 23 countries conducted by Michael North and Susan Fiske (2015), found just the opposite to be true. Considering these results and your own response, what factors do you think contribute to one's overall attitude toward growing older?

5. Do you think young adults' perceptions of growing old are accurate or inaccurate? Might perceptions of growing older be more accurate in some cultures than others? Please explain.

6. In many parts of the world, people do not keep track of birthdays or exact years of age. Would you expect attitudes toward aging to be any more or less favorable in that context?

Source

The Attitudes Toward Aging items were adapted with permission from:

Best, D. L., & Williams, J. E. Anticipation of aging: A cross-cultural examination of young adults' views of growing old. In J. Pandey, D. Sinha, & D. P. S. Bhawuk (Eds.), *Asian contributions to cross-cultural psychology*. Copyright © 1996 by Sage. Adapted with permission.

These items first appeared in:

Osteen, F. L. (1985). Aspects of subjective age and their relationship to physical, mental, and emotional well-being. Unpublished master's thesis. Wake Forest University.

References

Best, D. L., & Williams, J. E. (1996). Anticipation of aging: A cross-cultural examination of young adults' views of growing old. In J. Pandey, D. Sinha, & D. P. S. Bhawuk (Eds.), *Asian contributions to cross-cultural psychology* (pp. 274–288). Thousand Oaks, CA: Sage.

North, M. S., & Fiske, S. T. (2015). Modern attitudes toward older adults in the aging world: A cross-cultural meta-analysis. *Psychological Bulletin, 141*(5), 993–1021.

ACTIVITY 4.9
ETHNOGRAPHIC STUDIES OF HUMAN DEVELOPMENT

Carol and Melvin Ember (2001) suggested that making cross-cultural comparisons is impossible without ethnography. Ethnography provides detailed, culture-specific information that allows us to identify patterns and possible universals. Ethnography involves recording observations of daily behavior, generally over an extended period of time. Ethnographic researchers typically take in-depth notes on their observations and may work closely with knowledgeable members of the community they are studying. At times ethnographic researchers may even take part in the activities they are investigating, a technique called *participant observation.*

In a research technique called the *holocultural* or *hologeistic* method, hypotheses about the relationship between variables across cultures are typically tested using collections of ethnographies. In this form of research, societies rather than individuals are used as the unit of analysis. One of the most widely used collections of ethnographies is the Human Relations Area Files (HRAF). The HRAF databases (*eHRAF World Cultures* and *eHRAF Collection of Archeology*) contain ethnographies from over 400 cultural, ethnic, religious, and national groups around the world and have been used in hundreds of studies. For example, using the HRAF, Carol Ember, Teferi Abate Adem, and Ian Skoggard (2013) identified a link between climate-related disasters, such as drought, and the likelihood of warfare.

The following studies are examples of ethnographic research.

- Dina Birman and Nellie Tran (2017) spent two years conducting classroom observations and interviews to investigate how Somali Bantu refugee students adjusted to attending an elementary school in Chicago, U.S. They collected detailed accounts of the challenges faced by children and teachers. One outcome of this research was that they identified two different approaches that teachers took in dealing with cultural differences, an "assimilationist" approach, which emphasized a need for students to conform to U.S. culture and school rules, and a "multicultural" approach in which teachers showed respect for the students' expressions of their culture at school.
- Wai Han Lo (2017) attended Cantonese opera classes in Hong Kong as a participant observer and conducted interviews with the children enrolled. The class involved learning fighting moves and acting skills as well as Cantonese operatic songs. She reported that this experience resulted in a sense of achievement, ethnic identity, and personal growth for those involved.

The purpose of this activity is to become familiar with the method of ethnography, particularly as it informs our understanding of human development.

Directions: Using library resources, locate a published ethnography addressing some aspect of human development. Such studies focus on understanding the context of experiences and adaptations throughout the lifespan. The research article you select should describe a study conducted in a culture other than your own. Many social science books and journals include ethnographies. However, some particularly good journal sources for ethnographic accounts include:

- *American Anthropologist*
- *American Ethnologist*
- *American Journal of Sociology*
- *American Journal of Community Psychology*
- *Cross-Cultural Research*
- *Cultural Diversity and Ethnic Minority Psychology*
- *Culture & Psychology*
- *Current Anthropology*

- *Culture, Medicine, and Psychiatry*
- *Ethnic and Racial Studies*
- *Ethos*
- *Journal of Aging Studies*
- *Journal of Black Studies*
- *Journal of Comparative Family Studies*
- *Journal of Contemporary Ethnography*
- *Social Anthropology*
- *Social Science & Medicine*

After carefully reading your ethnography, answer the questions below. Be sure to attach a copy of your article to this worksheet.

1. In the space below, provide the full citation for your article (see the reference section of activities in this book for examples of the format and content of citations).

2. In your own words, describe the purpose of this ethnographic study.

3. Describe the ethnographic methods that were involved in this study.

4. Summarize the findings of the study. In what way did this research contribute to our understanding of human development?

5. What do you think might be some strengths and weaknesses of the ethnographic approach?

References

Birman, B. D., & Tran, N. (2017). When worlds collide: Academic adjustment of Somali Bantu students with limited formal education in a U.S. elementary school. *International Journal of Intercultural Relations, 60*, 132–144.

Ember, C. R., & Ember, M. (2001). *Cross-cultural research methods*. Lanham, MD: Rowman & Littlefield.

Ember, C. R., Adem, T. A., & Skoggard. I. (2013). Risk, uncertainty, and violence in eastern Africa: A cross-regional comparison. *Human Nature*, (24), 33–58.

Lo, W. H. (2017). Traditional opera and young people: Cantonese opera as personal development. *International Journal of Adolescence and Youth, 22*(2), 238–249.

ACTIVITY 4.10
TEXTBOOK REWRITE

As you learn more about culture and psychology you may find that you view your psychology lectures and reading materials from a new perspective. In fact, you may be tempted to fill in information about cultural variability or modify existing information to be more inclusive of diverse populations. This activity gives you an opportunity to do just that.

Directions:

1. Select a brief segment (one to two paragraphs) of a developmental psychology textbook or the developmental chapter of an introductory psychology textbook.
2. Use library resources or cross-cultural texts to locate material on cultural factors relevant to the aspect of development described in your text excerpt.
3. Rewrite the material so as to include the information about cultural influences. Be sure to make the appropriate citations for the material you include.
4. Include a copy of the original textbook passages with your rewrite.

The task of this activity involves not just adding information to the existing text passage, but significantly rewriting the material so as not to *marginalize* diverse perspectives. An example of this rewriting strategy is provided below.

Example

One way to start this process is to identify the emic or culture-specific information in the original, which is often presented as if universal (in the example below, the three socialization patterns are culture-specific). Then identify the etic, or universal construct (in the example, the universal concept is childrearing style). Be sure that your rewrite is built around the etic and not the emic.

Original

> Research based on Baumrind's (1971) model indicates that parents generally employ one of three socialization patterns: authoritarian, in which adults control children, permissive, in which there is little parental control, or authoritative socialization, in which parents set clear standards but also encourage independence.

Cultural influences included but marginalized

Research based on Baumrind's (1971) model indicates that parents generally employ one of three socialization patterns: authoritarian, in which adults control children, permissive, in which there is little parental control, or authoritative socialization, in which parents set clear standards but also encourage independence. However, these patterns may not apply to all ethnic groups. Chao (1994), for example, found that Baumrind's model did not fit Chinese parenting styles.

Inclusive rewrite

Childrearing styles vary across ethnic and cultural groups. Baumrind (1971) identified three main socialization patterns in research on European American parents: authoritarian, permissive, or authoritative parenting. Chao (1994) found that the concept of *chiao shun*, which emphasizes training children to know what is expected of them, best characterizes the parenting style of Chinese Americans.

In the space below provide the complete citation for the textbook you have selected and your inclusive rewrite.

References

Baumrind, D. (1971). Current patterns of parental authority. *Developmental Psychology Monographs, 4*(1), 1–103.

Chao, R. K. (1994). Beyond parental control and authoritarian parenting style: Understanding Chinese parenting through the cultural notion of training. *Child Development, 65,* 1111–1119.

–5–

Personality, Emotion, and the Self in Cultural Context

ACTIVITY 5.1
THE INTERDEPENDENT AND INDEPENDENT SELVES

One of the most researched topics in cross-cultural psychology is Hazel Markus and Shinobu Kitayama's (1991) self-construal theory. They posited that our sociocultural context shapes how we perceive our self – as interdependent and thus defined in terms of our relationships and inseparable from the social context, or as independent, focusing on how our individual traits, abilities, goals, and preferences distinguish us from others. They suggested that an interdependent self-construal would be more common in an East Asian cultural context and an independent self-construal would be more common among Westerners. According to Markus and Kitayama, the degree to which we hold an interdependent versus independent self-construal affects how we process thoughts, how we experience and express emotions, and how and when we are motivated. To date, there have been many challenges and revisions to the independent – interdependent framework, as well as scrutiny of the methods used in these studies, though it continues to be a topic of considerable research interest. This activity will familiarize you with the concept of self-construal.

Directions: Read each of the items in the two columns below and place a check next to the item in each pair that best describes you.

1. ____ Success depends on help from others. ____ Success depends on my abilities.

2. ____ I know more about others than I do about myself. ____ I know more about myself than I do about others.

3. ____ Being excluded from my group would be very hard on me. ____ Being dependent on others would be very hard on me.

4. ____ Silence is comfortable. ____ Silence is embarrassing.

5. ____ It is important that my behavior is appropriate for the situation. ____ It is important that my behavior and attitudes correspond.

6. ____ I sometimes feel ashamed. ____ I sometimes feel guilty.

7. ____ Friendships are difficult to establish but are generally very intimate. ____ Friendships are fairly easy to establish but often not very intimate.

8. ____ I generally socialize in groups. ____ I generally socialize in pairs.

____ **Total number of checks** ____ **Total number of checks**

---

1. The items in the column on the left indicate characteristics of the interdependent self, whereas items in the column on the right indicate characteristics of the independent self. According to the total number of checks for each column, is your self-construal more interdependent or independent? To what extent does your cultural background relate to this result?

2. It is possible that we each have both independent and interdependent self-construals. Harry Triandis (1994) suggested that individuals draw from different types of self-construal at any given moment depending on our cultural experiences and the situation. Describe below an instance in which you acted from an interdependent self-construal and one in which you acted from an independent self-construal.

Thinking Further

Studies have shown that it is possible to *prime* people to think independently or interdependently regardless of their cultural background. For example, participants may be asked to read one of two stories and count the number of pronouns (Brewer & Gardner, 1996). Those who read a story containing independent pronouns (e.g., *I, me, mine*) may act as if they have an independent self-construal and those who read a story containing interdependent pronouns (e.g., *we, us, our*) may act as if they have an interdependent self-construal. Several studies find differences in self-construal as a result of priming that are similar to those found when comparing Western and East Asian participants (Oyserman & Lee, 2008).

1. What do the results of priming studies tell us about how self-construal might develop?

2. Arzu Aydinli and Michael Bender (2015) have suggested that priming studies might help us to better understand multiculturalism. What might the results of priming studies mean for our ability to live in a multicultural society?

References

Aydinli, A., & Bender, M. (2015). Cultural priming as a tool to understand multiculturalism and culture. *Online Readings in Psychology and Culture, 2*(1), Article 13.

Brewer, M. B., & Gardner, W. L. (1996). Who is this "we"? Levels of collective identity and self representations. *Journal of Personality and Social Psychology, 71*, 83–93.

Markus, H., & Kitayama, S. (1991). Culture and self: Implications for cognition, emotion and motivation. *Psychological Review, 98*, 224–253.

Oyserman, D., & Lee, S. W. S. (2008). Does culture influence what and how we think? Effects of priming individualism and collectivism. *Psychological Bulletin, 134*(2), 311–342.

Triandis, H. C. (1994). *Culture and social psychology.* New York, NY: McGraw-Hill.

ACTIVITY 5.2
MULTIPLE AND SHIFTING IDENTITIES

There are many aspects of our identity in addition to culture. These different identities contribute to the diversity within cultural groups. This activity is designed to encourage you to examine your multiple group identities. Marshall Singer (1998) used the term *identity group* to refer to groups of people who perceive some aspect of the world similarly and who recognize and communicate about that similarity. According to Singer, the perceptions, values, attitudes, and beliefs that we learn from being a part of these groups, and the relative importance of our identity groups makes each of us unique.

Directions: Think for a minute about your identity groups; that is, the group memberships that most clearly define who you are. These may include gender, nationality, religion, socioeconomic status, race/ethnicity, sexual orientation, age cohort, disability status, as well as such affiliations as political party, academic discipline, occupation, hobbies, and sports teams. Then answer the questions below in the space provided.

1. List your identity groups below:

_____   _____

_____   _____

_____   _____

_____   _____

_____   _____

Go back to your list of identity groups above and rank them by putting a (1) next to the group that you identify with most strongly, a (2) next to the group that is next most important to you, and so on.

2. Did you find the groups difficult to rank? Why or why not?

3. One reason that identity groups may be difficult to rank is that their importance may vary with the situation. Describe below a situation in which an identity group that you ranked as relatively unimportant could be much more important to you.

4. Dimensions of identity do not exist in isolation but interact with each other to influence our life experiences and behavior. Kimberlé Crenshaw (1989) introduced the term *intersectionality* to refer to the overlapping forms of social injustice associated with identity. For example, the effects of ageism differ for men and women; the effects of growing up poor differ by race/ethnicity. What would happen if one of your primary identity groups changed – for example, your gender, socioeconomic class, race/ethnicity, or sexual orientation? Would this affect your other identity groups? If so how?

References

Crenshaw, K. (1989). Demarginalizing the intersection of race and sex: A Black feminist critique of antidiscrimination doctrine, feminist theory and antiracist politics. *University of Chicago Legal Forum, 1*. Retrieved from http://chicagounbound. uchicago.edu/uclf/vol1989/iss1/8

Singer, M. R. (1998). *Perception & identity in intercultural communication.* Yarmouth, ME: Intercultural Press.

ACTIVITY 5.3
MULTIRACIAL IDENTITY

The number of mixed race/ethnicity individuals is increasing markedly in many parts of the world. According to the Pew Research Center (2015) the number of multiracial infants born in the United States has tripled since 1980. The Pew survey found that the majority of multiracial adults are proud of their mixed-race background and feel their racial heritage has made them more open to other cultures. Maria Root (1998) conducted extensive research on the racial/ethnic identity of multiracial individuals. Some of her observations include the following:

- Individuals of mixed race/ethnicity are increasingly likely to identify themselves as racially/ethnically mixed.
- Racial/ethnic appearance does not predict racial/ethnic identity.
- An individual's racial/ethnic identity may change over time and across situations.
- Siblings of the same mixed heritage may have different racial/ethnic identities.

This activity deals with some of the many factors that influence racial/ethnic identity among individuals with multiracial heritage.

Directions: Please respond to each of the questions below in the space provided.

Imagine that you are the child of an Asian mother and a Black father. Describe how this racial/ethnic identity might change under the following conditions:

1. You live with your father only.

2. You live with your mother only.

3. Your appearance is of a Black person.

4. Your appearance is of an Asian person.

5. Your appearance is racially ambiguous.

6. You live in a predominantly Black neighborhood and have mostly Black friends.

7. You live in a predominantly Asian neighborhood and have mostly Asian friends.

8. You live in a racially mixed neighborhood and have friends from different ethnic and racial groups.

9. Your parents encourage knowledge of your ethnic and racial heritage.

10. Your parents rarely discuss issues of race or ethnicity.

11. Your family has experienced some anti-Black acts of discrimination.

12. Your family has experienced some anti-Asian acts of discrimination.

13. Your family has never experienced any discrimination.

14. You are male.

15. You are female.

Thinking Further

1. Discuss the relative importance of the factors listed above in terms of their contribution to ethnic/racial identity.

2. What other factors do you think might be relevant?

3. Maya Yampolsky, Catherine Amiot and Roxane de la Sablonnière (2016) found that individuals who are able to integrate their multiple cultural identities within their self-concept had greater well-being than those who focused on one predominant identity or who compartmentalized and maintained separate identities depending on the situation. Based on the different factors listed above, what types of experiences might facilitate multicultural identity integration?

References

Pew Research Center. (2015). *Multiracial in America: Proud, diverse and growing in numbers*. Washington, DC: Author.

Root, M. P. P. (1998). Experiences and processes affecting racial identity development: Preliminary results from the biracial sibling project. *Cultural Diversity and Ethnic Minority Psychology, 4*, 237–247.

Yampolsky, M. A., Amiot, C. E., & de la Sablonnière, R. (2016). The multicultural identity integration scale (MULTIIS): Developing a comprehensive measure for configuring one's multiple cultural identities within the self. *Cultural Diversity and Ethnic Minority Psychology, 22*(2), 166–184.

ACTIVITY 5.4
CULTURE AND TRAITEDNESS

Across cultures studied, people recognize the existence of individual personality traits and personality traits appear to be useful in predicting behavior, however there are cultural differences in traitedness, that is the extent to which people *believe* that their traits are stable and consistent. Numerous studies have found evidence for reduced traitedness in collectivistic cultures, especially East Asian cultures, as compared with individualist cultures. For example, Timothy Church and colleagues (2012) found that U.S. Americans, followed by Mexicans, were more likely to endorse these beliefs than were people from the Philippines and Japan. In addition, Velichko Fetvadjiev and colleagues (2018) found that more collectivist Black South Africans viewed their behavior as more variable than did more individualist White South Africans. In this activity you will explore your own level of traitedness and consider how traitedness may be related to other psychological phenomena.

Directions: Answer the questions below to assess your own level of traitedness.

1. Do you believe that your personality traits have been consistent over time? Please explain.

2. Do you believe that your personality traits have been consistent across situations? Please explain.

3. Do you believe that your personality traits can reliably predict your behavior? Please explain.

---

4. What do you conclude about your own level of traitedness?

Thinking Further

1. Helen Boucher (2011) reported lower traitedness among dialectical thinkers – individuals who are comfortable exploring and synthesizing contradictory ideas. How might you explain this finding?

2. Given that traitedness beliefs have been found to vary across cultures, how might the content and goals of psychological research differ in countries with low versus high traitedness?

References

Boucher, H. C. (2011). The dialectical self-concept II: Cross-role and within-role consistency, well-being, self-certainty, and authenticity. *Journal of Cross-Cultural Psychology, 42*(7), 1251–1271.

Church, A. T., Willmore, S. L., Anderson, A. T., Ochiai, M., Porter, N., Mateo, N. J., Reyes, J. A. S., de Jesús Vargas-Flores, J., Ibáñez-Reyes, J., Alvarez, J. M., Katigbak, M. S., & Ortiz, F. A. (2012). Cultural differences in implicit theories and self-perceptions of traitedness: Replication and extension with alternative measurement formats and cultural dimensions. *Journal of Cross-Cultural Psychology, 43*(8), 1268–1296.

Fetvadjiev, V. H., Meiring, D., van de Vijver, F., Nel, J. A., Sekaja, L., & Laher, S. (2018). Personality and behavior prediction and consistency across cultures: A multimethod study of Blacks and Whites in South Africa. *Journal of Personality and Social Psychology, 114*(3), 465–481.

ACTIVITY 5.5
RELIGION AND UNDERSTANDING CULTURE

In 2003, Nalini Tarakeshwar, Jeffrey Stanton, and Kenneth Pargament pointed out that religion is a much overlooked consideration in research on culture and psychology. In fact, their database search found that the percentage of articles dealing in some way with religion ranged from only 2% to just under 6% in cross-cultural journals. In the years since, the number of cross-cultural psychology publications addressing aspects of religion has increased markedly. For example, Silvia Gattino and colleagues (2016) investigated the role of religious identity for Muslim individuals who had immigrated to (predominantly Catholic) northern Italy. They found that although the strength of religious identification motivated the maintenance of Muslim culture, it was unrelated to the degree of acculturation to Italian culture. This activity will explore the role of religion in understanding the culture and human behavior.

Directions: For each of the aspects of culture listed below, give an example of how it may be related to one's religion. In order to do so, you may need to gather additional information about specific religions through discussions with others or library research.

1. Values

2. Child rearing practices

3. Health-related behaviors

---

4. Prejudice and stereotyping

5. Gender roles

6. Concept of the self

7. Beliefs about interpersonal relationships

8. Beliefs about education and learning.

Thinking Further

What do you conclude about the role of religion in cross-cultural research?

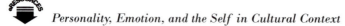

References

Gattino, S., Miglietta, A., Rizzo, M., & Testa, S. (2016). Muslim acculturation in a Catholic country: Its associations with religious identity, beliefs, and practices. *Journal of Cross-Cultural Psychology, 47*(9), 1194–1200.

Tarakeshwar, N., Stanton, J., & Pargament, K. I. (2003). Religion: An overlooked dimension in cross-cultural psychology. *Journal of Cross-Cultural Psychology, 34*, 377–394.

ACTIVITY 5.6
PUTTING EMOTIONS INTO WORDS

Across cultures, there is much similarity in the emotions people report experiencing, the events that trigger those emotions, and the subjective and physiological responses that accompany those emotions (Matsumoto & Hwang, 2013). Cultures differ, however, in how emotions are expressed, both verbally and nonverbally. A growing area of research focuses on lexicalized emotion, or how emotions are put into words (Ogarkova, 2013). One way that verbal expressions of emotion differ across cultures is the frequency with which somatic referents are used. Somatic referents are terms that express emotional states by referring to specific parts of the body. For example, emotion words used by the Hmong of Laos often refer to the liver, such as *term tu siab*, literally "broken liver" or sadness (Postert, Dannlowski, Müller, & Konrad, 2012). Many Persian emotion terms refer to the eye. For example, loving someone is expressed as "having place on one's eye" (Sharifian, 2011). In this activity you will investigate the frequency of somatic referents for emotion in your own language.

Directions: Follow the steps below to investigate somatic referents of emotion in your language. First, list words that label six different emotions in the column on the left. Then look up each word in a thesaurus and in the column on the right, list any somatic referents that appear for that term. For example, if you listed the term "disgust" on the left, you might find the somatic referent "stomach-turning" and list it on the right.

Basic Emotion Terms   Somatic Referents

- _____   _____
- _____   _____
- _____   _____
- _____   _____
- _____   _____
- _____   _____

1. Considering the words that appeared in the thesaurus for each of your emotion terms, did you find somatic referents to be frequent? Rare? Please explain.

2. Is there anything you can conclude from this analysis about the degree to which speakers of the language you investigated view mind and body as connected or separate? Please explain.

Thinking Further

1. Vivian Dzokoto and colleagues (2016), who identified a large number of somatic referents for emotions in two Ghanaian languages, suggested that somatic referents may be a way to express negative emotions in a manner that preserves social harmony. Why might this be the case?

2. How might cultural differences in the use of somatic referents to express emotions be relevant to counseling across cultures?

References

Dzokoto, V., Senft, N., Kpobi, L., & Washington-Nortey, P. (2016). Their hands have lost their bones: Exploring cultural scripts in two West African affect lexica. *Journal of Psycholinguistic Research, 45*(6), 1473–1497.

Matsumoto, D., & Hwang, H. S. (2013). Basic emotions. In K. Keith (Ed.), *Encyclopedia of cross-cultural psychology* (pp. 480–483). London, UK: Wiley-Blackwell.

Ogarkova, A. (2013). Folk emotion concepts: Lexicalization of emotional experiences across languages and cultures. In J. J. R. Fontaine, K. R. Scherer, & C. Soriano (Eds.), *Components of emotional meaning: A sourcebook* (pp. 46–62). Oxford, UK: Oxford University Press.

Postert, C., Dannlowski, U., Müller, J. M., & Konrad, C. (2012). Beyond the blues: Towards a cross-cultural phenomenology of depressed mood. *Psychopathology, 45*(3), 185–192.

Sharifian, F. (2011).Conceptualizations of *cheshm* "eye" in Persian. In Z. A. Maalej & N. Yu (Eds.), *Embodiment via body parts: Studies from various languages and cultures* (pp. 197–211). Amsterdam: John Benjamins.

ACTIVITY 5.7
CULTURAL DISPLAY RULES

Early studies by Paul Ekman and Wallace Friesen (Ekman, 1972) indicated that several emotions tend to be universal in that they can be recognized across cultures. Yet, there are marked cultural differences in when and how emotions are expressed. This is due in large part to variability in *cultural display rules*. According to David Matsumoto (2001), display rules are the guidelines one learns early in life about how to manage and modify the emotions you express, depending on the situation. For example, in one of the few studies of display rules conducted within Arab cultures, Sharon Flicker, Haneen Ayoub, and Melissa Guynn (2017) found that Palestinian students were more comfortable expressing powerless emotions (sadness and fear) to friends than parents. They suggest this may be due to greater comfort with friends or an effort to protect their parents from observing their emotional distress. This activity is designed to familiarize you with the concept of cultural display rules and to help you to identify the display rules you follow.

Directions: Over the next day or two, keep a record of your emotions and their expression. When you experience an identifiable emotion, make an entry below indicating when you experienced the emotion; the type of emotion you experienced (such as happiness, sadness, fear, anger, disgust or surprise); the setting in which you experienced the emotion (Were you alone or with others? Were you in a public or private place?); and the manner in which the emotion was expressed. (Indicate the form – such as laughing, yelling, or frowning – and the intensity of the expression). Try to record ten instances of emotional expression then answer the questions that follow.

	Date/Time	Emotion	Setting	Expression
1				
2				
3				
4				
5				

6				
7				
8				
9				
10				

1. Compare the instances of emotional expression that took place in private rather than public settings. What do you conclude about the display rules governing the public expression of emotion?

2. Compare the instances of emotional expression involving different types of emotions. Did you observe different rules governing the expression of positive (happiness, surprise) as opposed to negative (sadness, anger) emotions?

3. To what extent can you trace your display rules to your cultural background or gender socialization. Please explain.

Thinking Further

1. Several studies support an association between collectivism and lower levels of emotional expressivity (e.g., Matsumoto et al., 2008). Why do you think this might be so?

2. Adrienne Wood, Magdalena Rychlowska, and Paula Niedenthal (2016) have identified an additional predictor of emotional expressivity, historical heterogeneity, which refers to the number of source countries that have made up a country's present-day population over the last 500 years. Why might historical heterogeneity be associated with more expressive display rules?

3. How might cultural display rules affect the use of emoticons? One study (Park, Baek, & Cha, 2014) investigated emoticon usage patterns on Twitter in 78 countries and found that people in individualistic cultures were more likely to use mouth-oriented emoticons like :), whereas those in collectivistic cultures preferred eye-oriented emoticons like ^_^. Why might this be? [Hint: Think about how easy it is to express a wide range of emotions with your mouth as opposed to your eyes.]

References

Ekman, P. (1972). Universal and cultural differences in facial expression of emotion. In J. R. Cole (Ed.), *Nebraska symposium on motivation, 1971* (pp. 207–283). Lincoln, NE: University of Nebraska Press.

Flicker, S. M., Ayoub, H. J. S., & Guynn, M. J. (2017). Emotional display rules in Palestine: Ingroup/outgroup membership, status of interaction partner and gender. *International Journal of Psychology*. Advance online publication. doi: 10.1002/ijop.12429

Matsumoto, D. (2001). Culture and emotion. In D. Matsumoto (Ed.), *Handbook of culture and psychology* (pp. 171–194). New York, NY: Oxford University Press.

Matsumoto, D., Yoo, S. H., Fontaine, J., Anguas-Wong, A., Arriola, M., Ataca, B., . . . Grossi, E. (2008). Mapping expressive differences around the world: The relationship between emotional display rules and individualism versus collectivism. *Journal of Cross-Cultural Psychology, 39*(1), 55–74.

Park, J., Baek, Y. M., & Cha, M. (2014). Cross-cultural comparison of nonverbal cues in emoticons on twitter: Evidence from big data analysis. *Journal of Communication, 64*(2), 333–354.

Wood, A., Rychlowska, M., & Niedenthal, P. M. (2016). Heterogeneity of long-history migration predicts emotion recognition accuracy. *Emotion, 16*(4), 413–420.

ACTIVITY 5.8
DEAR SIGMUND (OR CARL)

Nearly all of the early personality psychology theorists came from a similar Western tradition in terms of the cultural values and assumptions inherent in their theories. This activity encourages you to think about these classical theories from a cross-cultural perspective.

Directions: Select the personality theory of either Sigmund Freud or Carl Rogers. Below, make some notes about important concepts in the theory you chose. Then write a one-page letter to one of these theorists in the space provided. In your letter, identify aspects of the theory that are culture bound and make recommendations for revision. For example, Freudian theory focuses on the role of the mother as primary caregiver, whereas in much of the world children are raised by multiple caregivers. Some suggestions are provided for concepts you might include in your consideration of each theory. It may also be helpful to refer to an introductory psychology or personality theories textbook for an overview of the theory you chose.

Freudian Theory – some concepts for cultural consideration: psychosexual stages; superego development; psychoanalysis; the use of projective tests.

Rogerian Theory – some concepts for cultural consideration: the self; unconditional positive regard; the fully functioning person; client-centered therapy.

Notes

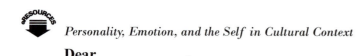

Dear_____,

ACTIVITY 5.9
THE CULTURE AND PERSONALITY
SCHOOL – OLD AND NEW

In the 1930s and 1940s, a major research focus of psychological anthropologists was the study of culture and personality. These studies were strongly influenced by Freudian research and often involved the use of psychoanalytic assessment tools (such as the Rorschach ink blots) to identify the basic personality type characterizing members of a specific culture. For example, in 1944 Cora DuBois published an analysis of the Alorese based on her extensive fieldwork in a small mountain village in the Dutch East Indies. In this book she discussed the connection between childrearing practices and adult character. Her data included ethnographic descriptions as well as the results of several psychological tests. She concluded that the structure of day-to-day activities led to the neglect of Alorese children and that this level of neglect resulted in such adult personality characteristics as emotional instability and distrust. DuBois' study typifies the culture and personality school. The purpose of this activity is to examine the assumptions underlying this significant area of research and to explore how, more than 80 years after the peak of the Culture and Personality School, some new research is using a different approach to once again ask whether cultural groups are characterized by specific personality types

Directions: Read, and then evaluate, each of the five assumptions of the Culture and Personality School stated below (adapted from Bock, 1995).

1. *The continuity assumption* – Early childhood experiences (such as weaning and toilet training) are the primary determinants of adult personality. Similar childhood experiences are assumed to result in similar adult personality types.
   Do you agree or disagree? Please explain.

2. *The uniformity assumption* – Societies can be described in terms of a core personality type. Along with this assumption is the idea that since childrearing behaviors are shaped by culture, they are fairly similar across families within a culture.
   Do you agree or disagree? Please explain.

---

3. *The causal assumption* – Basic personality structure is an entity that is not only observable but can cause, or be caused by, cultural institutions. For example, if a society is characterized as having a core personality trait of aggression, that trait can be described as causing a practice such as intergroup warfare. [Yet consider that the evidence for the core trait of aggression may come from observing such practices as intergroup warfare.]

   Do you agree or disagree? Please explain.

4. *The projective assumption* – By using projective tests (such as Rorschach ink blots) it is possible to determine basic personality characteristics and unconscious conflicts. Further, it is assumed that projective tests can be effectively used to understand the psychological makeup of an individual who is a member of a markedly different culture from the one in which the test was developed and standardized.

   Do you agree or disagree? Please explain.

5. *The objectivity assumption* – Cultural outsiders are able to accurately describe psychological characteristics and culturally patterned behaviors without imposing their own values or interpretations.

   Do you agree or disagree? Please explain.

Thinking Further

Rather than using projective tests, in recent decades national character has been studied by administering personality inventories to individuals in several countries and then comparing the aggregate scores for each country. For example, David Schmitt, Jüri Allik, Robert Mccrae and Verónica Benet-Martínez (2007) mapped personality profiles across 56 nations. Country-level personality scores have been found to correlate with Hofstede's dimensions (Individualism/Collectivism, Power Distance, Masculinity/Femininity, and Uncertainty Avoidance; Hofstede & McCrae, 2004), economic indicators (Stolarski, Zajenkowski, & Meisenberg, 2013), political regime type (Barceló, 2017), and the activities participants reported being engaged in at 7:00pm the previous evening (Baranski et al., 2017)! Yet, these between-country differences tend to be small and have not been consistent across studies. Furthermore, results show that within-country differences in personality are up to three times larger than between-country differences (Kajonius & Mac Giolla, 2017). Given the lack of evidence for large differences in personality across cultures, why do we have such strong stereotypes about people from specific countries?

Robert McCrae and colleagues (2013) investigated the association between national stereotypes and the personality test scores of individuals in 26 cultures. In line with the findings of previous studies of national stereotype accuracy, they reported a great deal of agreement about the traits people associated with each country, but these perceptions were not accurate in that they did not correspond to the actual measures of those traits. Please answer the questions below to explore these findings.

1. Describe a stereotype that you have or are familiar with about a country other than your own.

2. What might be the source of this stereotype, considering the extent to which there tends to be agreement about these perceptions?

---

3. What purpose might national stereotypes serve? In other words, why are they maintained?

4. How might these national stereotypes be harmful?

5. What forces might cause these national stereotypes to change over time?

Source

The five assumptions of the Culture and Personality School were adapted from Bock, P. K. *Rethinking psychological anthropology: Continuity and change in the study of human action.* Copyright © 1995 by Waveland Press. Adapted with permission.

References

Baranski, E. N., Gardiner, G., Guillaume, E., Aveyard, M., Bastian, B., Bronin, I., . . . Funder, D. C. (2017). Comparisons of daily behavior across 21 countries. *Social Psychological and Personality Science, 8*(3), 252–266.

Barceló, J. (2017). National personality traits and regime type: A cross-national study of 47 countries. *Journal of Cross-Cultural Psychology, 48*(2), 195–216.

Bock, P. K. (1995). *Rethinking psychological anthropology: Continuity and change in the study of human action.* Prospect Heights, IL: Waveland Press.

DuBois, C. (1944). *The people of Alor.* New York, NY: Harper & Row.

Hofstede, G., & McCrae, R. R. (2004). Personality and culture revisited: Linking traits and dimensions of culture. *Cross-Cultural Research, 38*, 52–88.

Kajonius, P., & Mac Giolla, E. (2017). Personality traits across countries: Support for similarities rather than differences. *PLoS ONE, 12*(6).

McCrae, R. R., Chan, W., Jussim, L., De Fruyt, F., Löckenhoff, C. E., De Bolle, M., . . . Terracciano, A. (2013). The inaccuracy of national character stereotypes. *Journal of Research in Personality, 47*(6), 831–842.

Schmitt, D. P., Allik, J., Mccrae, R. R., & Benet-Martínez, V. (2007). The geographic distribution of big five personality traits: Patterns and profiles of human self-description across 56 nations. *Journal of Cross-Cultural Psychology, 38*(2), 173–212.

Stolarski, M., Zajenkowski, M., & Meisenberg, G. (2013). National intelligence and personality: Their relationships and impact on national economic success. *Intelligence, 41*(2), 94–101.

ACTIVITY 5.10
ETIC AND EMIC APPROACHES TO PERSONALITY

A major goal of research in personality psychology is identifying etic, or universal, dimensions of personality. Studies conducted by different researchers using a variety of measures have found support for the existence of five basic personality traits (Costa & McCrae, 2006). These dimensions form the *Five Factor Model* (FFM). There is considerable cross-cultural evidence for the generality of the FFM traits (see, for example, Allik et al., 2017). However, the measures used to assess personality in these studies were developed primarily by researchers with a Western orientation to psychology and then translated and administered in other cultures, which creates the danger of an *imposed etic* (see Activity 2.3). In contrast, an emic, or culture-specific, approach to personality assessment has sought to identify indigenous dimensions of personality. For example, a series of studies by Timothy Church, Marcia Katigbak, and colleagues (e.g., Katigbak, Church, Guanzon-Lapeña, Carlota, & del Pilar, 2002) identified culture-specific dimensions of personality in the Philippines that added to the predictive power of the FFM. These include *Pagkamadaldal* (Social Curiosity), *Pagkamapagsapalaran* (Risk-taking), and religiosity. Fanny Cheung, Fons van de Vijver, and Frederick Leong (2011) advocated for a combined emic–etic approach in which, in addition to testing the universality of FFM traits across cultures, indigenously derived traits are tested for universality. These authors suggested that indigenous research could lead to the discovery of aspects of personality that have been overlooked by Western researchers due to "cultural blind spots." For example, both the indigenously derived Cross-cultural (Chinese) Personality Assessment Inventory (CPAI; Cheung, Cheung, & Fan, 2013) and the South African Personality Inventory (SAPI; Fetvadjiev, Meiring, van de Vijver, Nel, & Hill, 2015) may have identified universal dimensions of personality beyond those included in the FFM, including Interpersonal Relatedness. This activity will explore the combined emic–etic approach to better understanding this strategy for investigating personality across cultures.

Directions: There are three steps to this activity. First, in the column on the left side of the page, list ten traits or personality characteristics that describe you or someone you know. Second, read the descriptions of the FFM traits and indicate in the column on the right the FFM trait category under which each of the traits on the left would fall. If the trait on the left does not fit clearly into any of the FFM categories, then leave the corresponding FFM space blank. Finally, read about three indigenous personality traits and determine whether these fit under the FFM classifications.

Trait	FFM Category
1. _____	_____
2. _____	_____
3. _____	_____
4. _____	_____
5. _____	_____
6. _____	_____
7. _____	_____
8. _____	_____
9. _____	_____
10. _____	_____

The FFM (adapted from McCrae & Costa, 1997):

- *Openness* – Refers to the degree to which one is imaginative versus down-to-earth, prefers variety versus routine, and is independent versus conforming.
- *Conscientiousness* – Refers to the degree to which one is organized versus disorganized, careful versus careless, and self-disciplined versus weak willed.
- *Extraversion* – Refers to the degree to which one is sociable versus introverted, fun loving versus sober, and affectionate versus reserved.
- *Agreeableness* – Refers to the degree to which one is softhearted versus ruthless, trusting versus suspicious, and helpful versus uncooperative.
- *Neuroticism* – Refers to the degree to which one is worried versus calm, insecure versus secure, and self-pitying versus self-satisfied.

1. Listed below are three traits considered to be indigenous aspects of personality. Read the descriptions of these traits and determine which FFM category, if any, could be used to classify the trait.

Trait and Definition	**FFM Category**
• *Philotimo* (see Triandis & Vassiliou, 1972) involves being polite, generous, respectful, and meeting one's obligations. [Greek]	_____
• *Abnegation* (see Avendaño-Sandoval, Díaz-Guerrero & Reyes-Lagunes, 1997 cited in Fetvadjiev, Meiring, van de Vijver, Nel & Hill, 2015). The tendency to sacrifice oneself for others [Mexican]	_____
• *Amae* (see Doi, 1973) refers to a combination of childlike dependence on and obligation to another person. Rooted in the mother–child relationship, *amae* is also seen as characterizing the relationship between people of higher and lower status. [Japanese]	_____

2. Based on your findings, what do you conclude about the universality of the FFM?

Thinking Further

Discuss how the combined etic–emic approach could be used to investigate an area of psychology other than personality.

Source

The FFM descriptions were adapted from McCrae, R. R. & Costa, P. T. (1987). Validation of the five factor model of personality across instruments and observers. *Journal of Personality and Social Psychology, 52*, 81–90.

References

Allik, J., Church, A. T., Ortiz, F. A., Rossier, J., Hřebíčková, M., de Fruyt, F., Realo, A., & McCrae, R. R. (2017). Mean profiles of the NEO personality inventory. *Journal of Cross-Cultural Psychology, 48*(3), 402–420.

Cheung, F. M., van de Vijver, F. J. R., & Leong, F. T. L. (2011). Toward a new approach to the study of personality in culture. *American Psychologist, 66*(7), 593–603.

Cheung, F. M., Cheung, S. F., & Fan, W. (2013). From Chinese to cross-cultural personality inventory: A combined emic–etic approach to the study of personality in culture. In M. Gelfand, C. Y. Chiu, & Y. Y. Hong (Eds.), *Advances in culture and psychology* (Vol. 3, pp. 117–180). New York, NY: Oxford University Press.

Costa, P. T., & McCrae, R. R. (2006). Trait and factor theories. In J. C. Thomas, D. L. Segal, & M. Hersen (Eds.), *Comprehensive handbook of personality and psychopathology* (pp. 96–114). Hoboken, NJ: Wiley.

Doi, T. (1973). *The anatomy of dependence*. New York: Harper Row.

Fetvadjiev, V. H., Meiring, D., van de Vijver, F. J. R., Nel, J. A., & Hill, C. (2015). The South African Personality Inventory (SAPI): A culture-informed instrument for the country's main ethnocultural groups. *Psychological Assessment, 27*(3), 827–837.

Katigbak, M. S., Church, A. T., Guanzon-Lapeña, M. A., Carlota, A. J., & del Pilar, G. H. (2002). Are indigenous personality dimensions culture-specific? Philippine inventories and the five-factor model. *Journal of Personality and Social Psychology, 82*, 89–101.

McCrae, R. R., & Costa, P. T. (1987). Validation of the five factor model of personality across instruments and observers. *Journal of Personality and Social Psychology, 52*, 81–90.

Triandis, H. C., & Vassiliou, V. (1972). Comparative analysis of subjective culture. In H. C. Triandis (Ed.), *The analysis of subjective culture* (pp. 299–338). New York: Wiley.

Health, Stress, and Coping across Cultures

ACTIVITY 6.1
WHAT IS ABNORMAL?

Before exploring issues of culture and well-being, it is useful to consider what we mean when we talk about behavior that is normal or abnormal. This activity focuses on exploring these concepts.

Directions: Please respond to each of the questions below.

1. Describe a behavior that, within your culture, is/was considered abnormal at one point in history, but normal at another point in history.

2. Describe a behavior that, within your culture, is considered abnormal in one setting, but is considered normal in another setting.

3. Describe a behavior that is considered normal in your culture, but abnormal in some other culture(s).

4. Describe a behavior that is considered abnormal in your culture, but normal in some other culture(s).

---

5. Describe a behavior that is considered abnormal in all societies.

6. Develop a set of criteria that can be used to determine if a behavior is abnormal.

7. Would the criteria you developed likely apply across cultures? Please explain.

ACTIVITY 6.2
CULTURE AND HEALTH: THE NI HON SAN STUDY

Several studies of culture and health have taken advantage of what one might consider a natural experiment; that is, changes in health as a specific ethnic group migrates to another culture. By comparing the health measures of members of an ethnic group who do not migrate with those who do, we can begin to separate genetic from behavioral influences on health. An example of this type of research is the landmark Ni Hon San study described below. The purpose of this activity is to encourage you to think about how culturally embedded behaviors may influence health. In addition, this activity will familiarize you with a form of research that provides significant insights into issues of culture and health.

Directions: Read the description of the Ni Hon San study below (based on Benfante, 1992) and then answer the questions that follow.

The Ni Hon San Study

The Ni Hon San study began in 1964 as part of the Honolulu Heart Study and ran for over three decades. This research compared health data from three groups of men: Japanese men living in Hiroshima and Nagasaki, Japan; descendants of Japanese migrants to Hawaii; and descendants of Japanese migrants to San Francisco, California. One of the most striking findings of this study is that the rate of cardiovascular disease (heart disease) was lowest in the Japan group, highest in the California group, and intermediate in the Hawaii group.

1. What conclusions can you draw from the findings of the Ni Hon San study about the role of genetics and behavior in the development of cardiovascular disease?

2. What assumptions can you make about the distinction between individuals of Japanese ancestry living in Hawaii as opposed to California?

3. List some behavioral factors (things people do in daily life) that may have led to the findings of the Ni Hon San study.

4. List some environmental factors (aspects of the setting in which people live) that may have affected the findings of the Ni Hon San study.

5. The participants of the Ni Hon San study were all male. Would you have any concerns about extrapolating from this study to draw conclusions about the health practices of women? Why or why not?

Thinking Further

1. Since the conclusion of the Ni Hon San study, investigations of a number of other immigrant groups to the United States have found a disturbing pattern – the longer the amount of time spent in the U.S., the higher the risk of cardiovascular disease (Mooteri, Petersen, Dagubati, & Pai, 2004). This "immigrant paradox" has been found on a variety of physical and mental health measures with immigrants to Canada and European countries as well (Domnich, Panatto, Gasparini, & Amicizia, 2012). What actions might be taken to prevent this problem among people who immigrate?

2. Another example of long-term health research is the Adventist Health Studies, which have investigated health behaviors and risks among tens of thousands of Seventh-day Adventists over more than four decades (e.g., Fraser et al., 2015). The participants in these studies are from several ethnic groups but share the same set of dietary and lifestyle practices associated with the Adventist religion. How does this research design compare with that of the NI Hon San study? [Hint: Think about which variables are held constant and which vary.]

References

Benfante, R. (1992). Studies of cardiovascular disease and cause-specific mortality trends in Japanese-American men living in Hawaii and risk factor comparisons with other Japanese populations in the Pacific region: A review. *Human Biology, 64*, 791–805.

Domnich, A., Panatto, D., Gasparini, R., & Amicizia, D. (2012). The "healthy immigrant" effect: Does it exist in Europe today? *Italian Journal of Public Health, 9*(3), 1–7.

Fraser, G., Katuli, S., Anousheh, R., Knutsen, S., Herring, P., & Fan, J. (2015). Vegetarian diets and cardiovascular risk factors in black members of the Adventist Health Study-2. *Public Health Nutrition, 18*(3), 537–545.

Mooteri, S. N., Petersen, F., Dagubati, R., & Pai, R. G. (2004). Duration of residence in the United States as a new risk factor for coronary artery disease (The Konkani Heart Study). *American Journal of Cardiology, 93*, 359–361.

ACTIVITY 6.3
THE GLOBAL OBESITY EPIDEMIC

According to the World Health Organization (WHO, 2017) obesity rates have increased in every country in their database since 2010 and the global rate of obesity has more than doubled since 1980. In almost half of the Organization for Economic Co-operation and Development (OECD) countries, 50% or more of the population is overweight (OECD, 2017). This trend does not only affect adults; over 340 million of those 5 to19 years old are overweight or obese. Although high-income countries continue to have the highest prevalence, the rate at which obesity among children and adolescents is increasing is much faster in low and middle-income countries (WHO, 2017). These changes have resulted in devastating physical and mental health, economic, and societal consequences. This activity will help you to understand the sociocultural influences shaping the global obesity epidemic.

Directions: Investigate the rise of obesity in a specific country of your choice other than your own. Report your findings below on the statistics, causes, consequences, prevention efforts, and additional cultural factors involved. Sources of information on this topic include the websites of the World Health Organization (WHO; www.who.int) and the Organization for Economic Co-operation and Development (OECD; www.oecd.org) as well as academic journal and newspaper articles.

1. Country:

2. Statistics (e.g., percentage of adults and children who are obese; rate of increase):

3. Causes (e.g., poverty; increased exposure to fast food; decrease in physical activity due to changes in technology)

4. Consequences (e.g., high rates of diabetes, increased health care costs, greater employee absenteeism):

5. Prevention efforts (e.g., food labeling; mandated counseling and support sessions):

6. Additional cultural factors involved (e.g., norms against exercise for women in some cultures; an association of heavier weight with wealth in some developing nations):

References

Organization for Economic Co-operation and Development (OECD). (2017). *Obesity update* [Fact sheet]. Retrieved from www.oecd.org/health/obesity-update.htm

World Health Organization (WHO). (2017). *Obesity and overweight* [Fact sheet]. Retrieved from www.who.int/en/news-room/fact-sheets/detail/obesity-and-overweight

ACTIVITY 6.4
CULTURE AND MENTAL HEALTH QUIZ

In recent decades, there has been a rapid increase in research on issues of culture and mental health. This activity will enable you to test your knowledge of a variety of key findings from this literature.

Directions: Decide whether each of the statements below is true or false. Then check your answers at the back of this book.

1. Depression and schizophrenia appear to be universal in that these mental illnesses have been found across cultures studied.

   TRUE / FALSE

2. The likelihood of recovering from schizophrenia is greater for patients in industrialized nations than in developing societies.

   TRUE / FALSE

3. Across cultures, there is no consistent gender difference in rates of autism.

   TRUE / FALSE

4. A syndrome widely recognized in Japan is a form of work-related stress that translates as "death by overwork."

   TRUE / FALSE

5. Anorexia nervosa, a syndrome marked by self-starvation and a distorted body image, is specific to the relatively affluent cultures of North America and Europe.

   TRUE / FALSE

6. Across cultures studied, most therapists surveyed agree that successful treatment for alcohol abuse requires complete abstinence from drinking.

   TRUE / FALSE

7. Clients are less likely to drop out of therapy if they are paired with a therapist of their own race/ethnicity.

   TRUE / FALSE

8. Attention Deficit Hyperactivity Disorder (ADHD) does not exist in some cultures.

   TRUE / FALSE

9. When seeking help, people of Chinese heritage tend to emphasize somatic (or physical), rather than psychological, symptoms of mental Illness. TRUE / FALSE

10. In addition to affecting the well-being of those targeted, racism also affects the well-being of those holding racist beliefs. TRUE / FALSE

ACTIVITY 6.5
SUBJECTIVE WELL-BEING ACROSS CULTURES

In recent decades, thousands of studies across the globe have investigated subjective well-being and over 40 countries have implemented a mechanism for assessing the subjective well-being of their citizens. Subjective well-being (SWB) has been defined as ". . . a person's cognitive and affective evaluations of his or her life" (Diener, Lucas, & Oishi, 2005, p. 63). Thus, SWB involves the way people think about their own life satisfaction (the cognitive component) and their general mood and emotions (the affective component). Some measures of SWB have simply asked people to rate their overall level of happiness, whereas others have involved self-report questionnaires, sampling people's real-time experiences, asking people to reconstruct their prior day, measuring brain activity, and analyzing the use of positive and negative emotion words on the Internet (Myers & Diener, 2018, p. 218). SWB comparisons have been made both on an individual level and on a national level. The purpose of this activity is to learn about SWB while assessing common beliefs about its determinants.

Directions: Administer the following questionnaire to three individuals to learn about their beliefs about SWB, then respond to the questions that follow.

Participant A

1. Throughout the world, are women happier than men, men happier than women, or is there no difference? Please explain your answer.

2. Are people happier in rich countries or poor countries? Please explain your answer.

---

3. Is self-esteem related to happiness? Please explain your answer.

Participant B

1. Throughout the world, are women happier than men, men happier than women, or is there no difference? Please explain your answer.

2. Are people happier in rich countries or poor countries? Please explain your answer.

3. Is self-esteem related to happiness? Please explain your answer.

Participant C

1. Throughout the world, are women happier than men, men happier than women, or is there no difference? Please explain your answer.

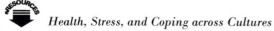

2. Are people happier in rich countries or poor countries? Please explain your answer.

3. Is self-esteem related to happiness? Please explain your answer.

After reading the research findings below, indicate which of your respondents' answers were accurate and which were inaccurate. Discuss the possible source of any inaccurate beliefs.

- Women and men report similar levels of life satisfaction and happiness. In their analysis of Gallup World Poll data, Ed Diener and Louis Tay found that gender was a poor predictor of life satisfaction, with men scoring higher in 72 nations and women scoring higher in 76 nations (detailed in Myers & Diener, 2018). In countries where significant gender differences in SWB exist, they seem to be associated with women's lack of access to resources and opportunities (Tesch-Römer, Motel-Klingebiel, & Tomasik, 2008).
- People are generally happier in wealthy than poor countries. This may be due to some common characteristics of wealthier nations, such as political stability, lack of ethnopolitical conflict, educational opportunities, and better health (Myers & Diener, 2018).
- Self-esteem tends to be more strongly associated with SWB in Western cultures than in East Asian cultures. One explanation for this is that high self-esteem is more useful in individualistic Western societies where there is greater relational mobility (people more frequently join new groups and leave old ones) than in more collectivist East Asian societies (Yuki, Sato, Takemura, & Oishi, 2013).

Thinking Further

1. Review the methods used to measure SWB that are described at the beginning of this activity. To what extent do you think cross-cultural differences in assessed SWB is a result of the methods used rather than actual differences in SWB? [Consider, for example, whether culture or language might affect the cognitive and affective components of SWB or how participants from different countries perceive the terms researchers use to refer to SWB.]

2. Monitoring levels of SWB is important since people with higher SWB : "tend to be healthier and longer-lived, thanks to a stronger immune system, better cardiovascular health, and healthier behaviors (exercising, wearing seat belts, even using sun screen); have better relationships, have more friends, more often get and stay married, and rate their marriages as better; are more prosocial and are engaged organizational citizens; and succeed more at work" (Myers & Diener, 2018, p. 224).

   Fortunately, it is possible to increase SWB on both an individual and societal level. SWB has been shown to increase over time with better social support, safety, human rights, environmental quality and green spaces, and income security and employment (Diener, Oishi, & Lucas, 2015). In the space below, describe a specific intervention that could be implemented to increase SWB in your community.

References

Diener, E., Lucas, R. E., & Oishi, S. (2005). Subjective well-being: The science of happiness and life satisfaction. In C. R. Snyder & S. J. Lopez (Eds.), *Handbook of positive psychology (2nd ed.)*, (pp. 63–73). New York, NY: Oxford University Press.

Diener, E., Oishi, S., & Lucas, R. E. (2015). National accounts of subjective well-being. *American Psychologist, 70*(3), 234–242.

Myers, D. G., & Diener, E. (2018). The scientific pursuit of happiness. *Perspectives on Psychological Science, 13*(2), 218–225.

Tesch-Römer, C., Motel-Klingebiel, A., & Tomasik, M. J. (2008). Gender differences in subjective well-being: Comparing societies with respect to gender equality. *Social Indicators Research, 85*(2), 329–349.

Yuki, M., Sato, K., Takemura, K., & Oishi, S. (2013). Social ecology moderates the association between self-esteem and happiness. *Journal of Experimental Social Psychology, 49*(4), 741–746.

ACTIVITY 6.6
CLIMATE CHANGE AND MENTAL HEALTH

A relatively new and concerning area of cross-cultural research deals with the current and potential psychological effects of climate change. Helen Louise Berry, Kathryn Bowen, and Tord Kjellstrom (2010) have outlined the direct and indirect pathways through which climate change may affect mental health. Direct effects involve the psychological trauma associated with exposure to more frequent and intense climate-related disasters, such as drought, floods, hurricanes, and fires. Indirect effects stem from threats to physical health, such as increased vulnerability to disease and disruption to food supply, as well as from economic and social threats to one's community, such as loss of property, income, and social support. The purpose of this activity is to add to our understanding of the connection between climate change and mental health across cultures.

Directions: For this activity you are asked to search a psychology database (such as PsycINFO) to locate a journal article reporting research on climate change and mental health and then to identify variables that could help us to understand this relationship. For example, here are three variables to consider:

- Individualism/Collectivism – Research in China found that respondents who scored high on individualism were less likely to support policies to mitigate climate change (Xue, Hine, Marks, Phillips, & Zhao, 2016).
- Cultural norms for expression of distress – Droughts and crop failures have led to large numbers of suicides among farmers in central India (Sen, Dhimal, Latheef, & Ghosh, 2017).
- Gender – Research in Fiji, Cyprus, New Zealand, and the United Kingdom found that women may be at greater risk for the effects of climate change due to their role in agricultural work and greater financial vulnerability (Du Bray, Wutich, Larson, White, & Brewis, 2018).

1. In the space below, provide the full citation for your article (see the reference section of activities in this book for examples of the format and content of citations).

---

2. Describe a variable addressed in your article that should be considered in research on climate change and mental health across cultures. Be sure to detail the evidence for the importance of that variable.

References

Berry, H. L., Bowen, K., & Kjellstrom, T. (2010). Climate change and mental health: A causal pathways framework. *International Journal of Public Health, 55*, 123–132

Du Bray, M., Wutich, A., Larson, K. L., White, D. D., & Brewis, A. (2018). Anger and sadness: Gendered emotional responses to climate threats in four island nations. *Cross-Cultural Research*. Advance online publication. doi: 10.1177/1069397118759252

Sen, B., Dhimal, M., Latheef, A. T., & Ghosh, U. (2017). Climate change: Health effects and response in South Asia. *BMJ : British Medical Journal, 359*. Advance online publication. doi: 10.1136/bmj.j5117.

Xue, W., Hine, D. W., Marks, A. D. G., Phillips, W. J., & Zhao, S. (2016). Cultural worldviews and climate change: A view from China. *Asian Journal of Social Psychology, 19*(2), 134–144.

ACTIVITY 6.7
CULTURAL CONCEPTS OF DISTRESS

It has long been clear that culture shapes the way people experience, explain, label, and treat mental disorders. According to Junko Tanaka-Matsumi (2001), researchers have taken two major approaches to understanding cultural differences in mental disorders. One approach, the *universalist* view, holds that there exist similarities in disorders across cultures, but the expression of these disorders differs from culture to culture. A second perspective, the *cultural relativist* approach, suggests that some disorders are unique to specific cultures and may only be understood within the context of those cultures.

Many clusters of symptoms that appear throughout the world do not clearly map onto Western categories of mental disorders such as those described in the *Diagnostic and Statistical Manual of Mental Disorders* (DSM) published by the American Psychiatric Association. These clusters of symptoms were once referred to as *culture-specific disorders* or *culture-bound syndromes*. However, this designation was problematic because it implied that these disorders are atypical and exotic whereas the disorders experienced in Western industrialized nations are universal and uninfluenced by culture. The DSM (DSM-5; 2013) now reflects the current view among mental health researchers that mental disorders involve both etic (universal) and emic (culture-specific) components. In addition, it no longer uses terms like *culture-specific disorders* or *culture-bound syndromes* and instead provides information on three aspects of cultural concepts of distress: cultural syndromes, cultural idioms of distress, and cultural explanations. We will explore each of these below.

Directions: Choose a cultural concept of distress to investigate using library or Internet resources (an appendix of the DSM-5 also includes detailed descriptions of cultural concepts of distress). Several cultural concepts of distress are listed below, though you may discover others in your search. Before you start, read through the questions that follow and be prepared to address these with the information you gather.

- ataque de nervios
- dhat syndrome
- khyâl cap
- kufingisisa
- maladi moun
- nervios
- shenjing shuairuo
- susto

1. Identify the cultural concepts of distress you selected as well as the location(s) in which it occurs:

2. Describe the cultural syndrome – the clusters of symptoms that tend to occur in a specific cultural group, community, or context.

3. Describe the cultural idiom of distress – the way people express or communicate their emotional suffering.

4. Describe the cultural explanation for this mental illness – the way that the cause or origin of the disorder is explained within the specific culture.

5. All mental disorders can best be understood as having both etic (universal) and emic (culture-specific) aspects. For example, Lisa Marie Beardsley (1994) mapped the etic and emic symptoms of *taijin-kyofusho,* a type of social phobia found in Japan. In this disorder, patients, primarily males, become fearful that they will offend others by such acts as staring, blushing, or emitting odors.

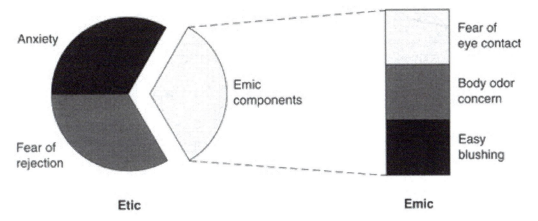

Source: Beardsley (1994).

In the space provided below, diagram the emic and the etic components of the cultural concept of distress that you investigated.

Thinking Further

Juris Draguns (1973) observed that the expression of mental disorders within a specified culture tends to be an *exaggeration of the normal*. In the case of *taijin-kyofusho*, the symptoms expressed indicate an exaggeration of the Japanese value of sensitivity toward others (Tanaka-Matsumi & Draguns, 1997). Consider the cultural context of the disorder you investigated. Can this disorder be viewed as an exaggeration of the normal? Please explain.

Source

Figure reprinted from Beardsley, L. M. Medical diagnosis and treatment across cultures. In W. J. Lonner & R. S. Malpass (Eds.), *Psychology and culture* (pp. 279–284). Copyright © 1994 by Allyn & Bacon. Reprinted with permission.

References

American Psychiatric Association. (2013). *Diagnostic and Statistical Manual of Mental Disorders* (5th ed.). Arlington, VA: American Psychiatric Publishing.

Beardsley, L. M. (1994). Medical diagnosis and treatment across cultures. In W. J. Lonner & R. S. Malpass (Eds.), *Psychology and culture* (pp. 279–284). Boston, MA: Allyn & Bacon.

Draguns, J. (1973). Comparison of psychopathology across cultures: Issues, findings, directions. *Journal of Cross-Cultural Psychology, 4*, 9–47.

Tanaka-Matsumi, J. (2001). Abnormal psychology and culture. In D. Matsumoto (Ed.), *Handbook of culture and psychology* (pp. 265–86). New York, NY: Oxford University Press.

Tanaka-Matsumi, J., & Draguns, J. (1997). Culture and psychopathology. In J. W. Berry, M. H. Segall, & C. Kagitcibasi (Eds.), *Handbook of cross-cultural psychology: Vol. 3* (2nd ed., pp. 449–491). Boston, MA: Allyn & Bacon.

ACTIVITY 6.8
SELF-HELP AND CULTURAL IDEALS

According to Daniel Nehring and colleagues (Nehring, Alvarado, Hendriks, & Kerrigan, 2016), a multi-billion dollar self-help industry is sweeping countries across the globe. Self-help books, podcasts, and websites provide advice on actions individuals can take to solve personal problems and have a more fulfilling life. They also provide clues about cultural ideals. This activity explores how well-being is viewed in a dominant culture by examining popular self-help books.

Directions: For this activity you will need to visit your local bookstore or public library and investigate the self-help section, sometimes labeled "Psychology" or "Self-Improvement." (You could also complete this activity using an online bookstore if you are able to look inside and at the back cover of the books.) Spend some time looking at a good sampling of self-help books and then answer the questions below.

1. Based on the self-help books you examined, list five authors/titles of books addressing the well-being of women. Explain how you decided that women are the intended audience.

2. Based on the self-help books you examined, list five authors/titles of books addressing the well-being of men. Explain how you decided that men are the intended audience.

3. Was it easier to find self-help books targeting women or men? Please explain.

4. List the authors/titles of any self-help books that support individualist goals (such as independence, assertiveness, or individual achievement).

5. List the authors/titles of any self-help books that support collectivist goals (such as family harmony, fulfilling obligations to others, or working as a team).

6. Was it easier to find self-help books targeting individualist or collectivist goals? Please explain.

7. You may find that self-help books tend to address the well-being of some groups and ignore others. List some topics that you would add to make the collection of self-help books more inclusive of diverse readers and issues.

8. Based on your examination of self-help books, what characteristics or abilities would one need in order to achieve well-being? Do these requirements for well-being differ by gender? Please explain.

Thinking Further

Consider for a moment the concept of self-help book. What cultural values underlie this phenomenon? For example, culture may shape our ideas about the best sources of advice or about the ability of individuals to change the direction of their lives.

Reference

Nehring, D., Alvarado, E., Hendriks, E. C., & Kerrigan, D. (2016). *Transnational popular psychology and the global self-help industry: The politics of contemporary social change*. London, UK: Palgrave Macmillan.

ACTIVITY 6.9
CLIENT'S AND COUNSELOR'S THOUGHTS

In the decades since the first publications on race, culture, and counseling in the mid-1970s, multicultural competence and social justice training have become central to counselor education and certification. Pamela Hays (2001) suggested that it is important for counselors to examine their own biases and inexperience regarding cultural and social groups. Her *ADDRESSING* model focuses on the interacting cultural influences of **A**ge, **D**evelopmental and acquired **D**isability, **R**ace, **E**thnicity, **S**ocial status, **S**exual orientation, **I**ndigenous heritage, **N**ational origin, and **G**ender. Some approaches to training practitioners of multicultural counseling, such as Paul Pedersen's (1994; 2000) Triad Model, use role plays in which participants other than those enacting the client and counselor make the cultural issues explicit. This activity, based on these approaches, encourages you to consider some of the complexities of multicultural counseling and the preparation of counselor trainees for intercultural interaction.

Directions: For this activity you are asked to write two versions of a scenario that illustrates cultural differences between a client and counselor. The first version should consist of a dialogue between a client and a counselor in which there is some cultural misunderstanding or misperception that is NOT verbalized. In the second version, make the cultural issues explicit by including the thoughts of the client and of the counselor (see the example below). Be sure that you use this activity as an opportunity to dispel – rather than create – stereotypes. It is also important to remember that there is a great deal of variability within any social group, and the cultural differences illustrated in this activity should be thought of as illustrating dimensions on which *cultures* may differ, but not a guide for determining the behavior or attitudes of particular *individuals*. The example below addresses age as a factor in a client-counselor interaction.

Before you begin, read the following example as a class, with student volunteers assigned to the four parts.

Example

The following is a counseling session involving a 32-year-old male psychotherapist, Dr. Allen, and a 70-year-old female client, Mrs. Green.

Counselor: Come right in, Mrs. Green, I hope I haven't kept you waiting long.
Client: That's quite alright, I brought something to do in the waiting room.
Counselor: Well, fine. Now tell me why you've come to see me today.

Client:	Well, I've been having some trouble with my mind.
Counselor:	What do you mean, Mrs. Green?
Client:	I guess it might be called "writer's block," but it's been going on for some time now and I'm rather concerned about it.
Counselor:	Now when did you first realize you were having trouble with your memory?
Client:	Uh . . . um . . . it's not my memory exactly . . . um it's more like my ability to generate creative new ideas in my writing. You see, after I retired from teaching I took up writing novels and uh . . .
Counselor:	Mrs. Green, maybe you need some other activities. There's a crafts class right here at the clinic on Thursdays.
Client:	Well, maybe I'll check into it.
Counselor:	In the meantime, let's make an appointment for the same time next week.
Client:	That should be fine, Dr. Allen. See you then.

The second version of the scenario includes the thoughts of the client and counselor:

The following is a counseling session involving a 32-year-old male psychotherapist, Dr. Allen, and a 70-year-old female client, Mrs. Green.

Counselor:	Come right in, Mrs. Green, I hope I haven't kept you waiting long.
[Counselor's Thoughts:	I hope I haven't made her cranky or anything.]
Client:	That's quite alright, I brought something to do in the waiting room.
[Counselor's Thoughts:	Oh, that bag must be full of knitting or needlepoint.]
[Client's Thoughts:	Good thing I brought my manuscript to work on. I had no idea I'd have to wait for such a long time.]
Counselor:	Well, fine. Now tell me why you've come to see me today.
[Counselor's Thoughts:	I guess this isn't going to be one of my most exciting mornings.]
Client:	Well, I've been having some trouble with my mind.
Counselor:	What do you mean, Mrs. Green?
[Counselor's Thoughts:	Oh no, could be Alzheimer's!]
Client:	I guess it might be called "writer's block," but it's been going on for some time now and I'm rather concerned about it.
Counselor:	Now when did you first realize you were having trouble with your memory?

[*Counselor's Thoughts*:	Talk about memory problems . . . I can't seem to recall what I learned in graduate school about the diagnostic criteria for dementia.]
Client:	Uh . . . um . . . it's not my memory exactly . . . um it's more like my ability to generate creative new ideas in my writing.
[*Client's Thoughts*:	I get it! He thinks I'm senile!]
Client:	You see, after I retired from teaching I took up writing novels and uh . . .
[*Client's Thoughts*:	He's looking at me like I'm crazy. This is so unnerving.]
[*Counselor's Thoughts*:	Hmm . . . she forgot the end of her sentence. Not a good sign in terms of cognitive functioning.]
Counselor:	Mrs. Green, maybe you need some other activities . . . there's a crafts class right here at the clinic on Thursdays.
[*Counselor's Thoughts*:	She just needs to stay busy.]
Client:	Well, maybe I'll check into it.
[*Client's Thoughts*:	He doesn't understand my situation at all. I guess it was a big mistake to go to a counselor.]
Counselor:	In the meantime, let's make an appointment for the same time next week.
[*Counselor's Thoughts*:	I guess I should get her back to make a more thorough diagnosis of her memory deficits.]
Client:	That should be fine, Dr. Allen. See you then.
[*Client's Thoughts*:	I'll call and cancel the appointment as soon as I get home.]

Write your dialogue (without client or counselor thoughts) in the space below:

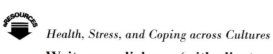

Write your dialogue (with client and counselor thoughts) in the space below:

References

Hays, P. A. (2001). *Addressing cultural complexities in practice: A framework for clinicians and counselors*. Washington, DC: American Psychological Association.

Pedersen, P. (1994). Simulating the client's internal dialogue as a counselor training technique. *Simulation and Gaming, 25*, 40–50.

Pedersen, P. B. (2000). *A handbook for developing multicultural awareness* (3rd ed.). Alexandria, VA: American Association for Counseling and Development.

ACTIVITY 6.10
CULTURE AND PSYCHOTHERAPY

This exercise will explore the ways in which your conception of therapy may be culture bound and will help you to better understand one *indigenous* form of psychotherapy.

Directions: Use the space provided to respond to the questions below.

1. You are probably familiar with the use of psychotherapy to treat emotional or psychological difficulties. You may have read about therapy, seen therapists in the media, may know someone who has been to a therapist, or may have been to a therapist yourself. Based on your perceptions, please define the term "therapy" below.

2. List some of the major features of therapy.

In the 1920s, a Japanese psychiatrist name Shoma Morita developed a therapy to treat neuroses that is based in part on Buddhist principles. Morita therapy is part of the foundation for a form of treatment popular in Europe and North America called *Constructive Living* (Tanaka-Matsumi, 2004). Morita focuses on rest and isolation. In fact, David Reynolds (1976) observed a sign in one Morita clinic that read "People who converse will not get well." The therapy generally lasts from four to eight weeks and consists of the following stages (as outlined by Prince, 1980, p. 299):

a. Total bed rest and isolation for 4 to 10 days; the patient is totally inactive and not permitted to converse, read, write, or listen to the radio.
b. For the next 7 to 14 days, the patient is out of bed and allowed to do light work in the garden; the patient begins to write a diary for the doctor but other human contact is forbidden.

---

c. For a further week or two the patient is instructed to do heavier work, continue the diary, and attend lectures from the doctor on self-control, the evils of egocentricity, and so forth.

d. Finally, the patient gradually returns to full social life and his former occupation; the patient continues contact with the doctor and attends group sessions with other patients on an out-patient basis.

3. How do you think you would feel as a patient of Morita therapy?

4. Contrast Western psychotherapy and Morita therapy. How are they different?

5. Compare Western psychotherapy and Morita therapy. How are they the same?

6. Revise your definition of therapy to include both Morita therapy and Western psychotherapy. [Hint: focus on the *function* rather than the *process* of therapy.]

References

Prince, R. (1980). Variations in psychotherapeutic procedures. In H. C. Triandis & J. Draguns (Eds.), *Handbook of cross-cultural psychology: Vol. 6. Psychopathology* (pp. 291–349). Boston, MA: Allyn & Bacon.

Reynolds, D. K. (1976). *Morita therapy.* Berkeley, CA: University of California Press.

Tanaka-Matsumi, J. (2004). Japanese forms of psychotherapy: Naikan therapy and Morita therapy. In U. P. Gielen, J. M. Fish, & J. G. Draguns (Eds.), *Handbook of culture, therapy, and healing* (pp. 277–291). Mahwah, NJ: Erlbaum.

Culture and Social Behavior

ACTIVITY 7.1
VIOLATING CULTURAL NORMS

Social norms are (often unspoken) rules or expectations about how people within a given group should behave. Social psychologists have found that people generally choose to conform to the social norms of the groups to which they belong. This activity explores the importance of the content and strength of social norms in defining a culture.

Directions: The statements below will instruct you to list social norms, choose one of these norms to violate, and then answer a series of questions based on your experience.

1. Examples of social norms relevant to some cultures include:

   - Forming a line when a group of people are waiting.
   - Applauding when a performance is completed.
   - Saying "excuse me" if you bump into strangers in a crowded place.

   In the space provided, list five social norms that you have observed.

2. Choose one of the norms you listed above to violate. Please be sure that your behavior is not illegal and does not put you or others in any danger. Your norm violation need not be anything very dramatic. Sometimes we can learn more by subtle than drastic norm violations.

   In the space below, describe your violation of a social norm, including (a) the setting, (b) the nature of the norm violation, (c) how you felt during the norm violation, and (d) how others responded to your behavior.

3. Discuss the cultural value that underlies the norm you chose to violate.

4. Why do you think we generally conform to the social norms of our culture?

5. Why do you think we typically react negatively toward those who violate our social norms?

6. Have you ever inadvertently violated a social norm? Please explain.

7. How did you learn the social norms of your own culture?

8. How would you go about learning the social norms of an unfamiliar culture?

Thinking Further

Perrti Pelto (1968) distinguished between loose cultures, which have weaker social norms and greater tolerance for deviance, and tight cultures, which have strong norms and severe punishments for their violation. Michele Gelfand, Jesse Harrington, and Joshua Jackson (2017) explained the evolution of looseness-tightness in terms of threat. They suggested that in societies with a history of social and ecological threats (e.g., lack of resources, natural disasters, disease, warfare), strong norms evolved to facilitate coordinated action. Several Asian nations were among the tightest of those measured and several Eastern European nations were among the loosest (Gelfand et al., 2011).

How might someone from a loose culture experience life in a tight culture? How do you think someone from a tight culture would experience life in a loose culture?

References

Gelfand, M. J., Harrington, J. R., & Jackson, J. C. (2017). The strength of social norms across human groups. *Perspectives on Psychological Science, 12*(5), 800–809.

Gelfand, M. J., Raver, J. L., Nishii, L., Leslie, L. M., Lun, J., Lim, B. C., . . . Aycan, Z. (2011). Differences between tight and loose cultures: A 33-nation study. *Science, 332,* 1100–1104.

Pelto, P. J. (1968). The differences between "tight" and "loose" societies. *Society, 5*(5), 37–40.

ACTIVITY 7.2
SHOPPING FOR CULTURAL VALUES

Sometimes it is easier to identify the cultural values of groups that are more foreign to us than to identify cultural values that permeate our day to day environment. Cultural values have been studied in a wide variety of settings including hospitals, schools, businesses, sports events, coffee shops, and children's birthday parties. This activity is designed to give you some perspective on the cultural values in your community through a trip to your neighborhood supermarket or grocery store.

Directions: Select a supermarket or grocery store in your community. Plan to spend 30 minutes to an hour making your observations. Take careful notes about the shoppers, the products available for purchase, and the layout of the store so that you can answer the questions below.

Name of store _____

Type of store _____

Time of day _____

1. What type of food or products were most plentiful in the store? What type of food or products were scarce?

2. What claims were used to promote food items? Did these claims emphasize taste, nutritional value, cost, ease of preparation?

3. What were the most expensive items in the store? When a wide range of prices exists for the same type of product, what distinguished the lower from the higher-cost versions?

4. What type of behavior did you observe on the part of the shoppers? Under what circumstances did shoppers interact with each other?

5. How were meats and poultry packaged? Were they labeled and displayed in a way that distances these products from their original animal form? Please explain.

6. What did you observe about the sizes in which different types of products were available? What did these sizes imply about the social settings in which the products will be used? For example, did you see more individual servings or family size packaging?

7. How were foods from various ethnic groups distributed throughout the store? Were some foods presented as normative (integrated throughout the store) whereas others were placed in a separate section or presented as unusual or exotic?

8. What other observations did you make that informed you about cultural values?

9. Based on your answers to the questions above, what cultural values were evident in the supermarket setting?

Thinking Further

Shalom Schwartz and colleagues have conducted extensive cross-cultural research on values. These studies support the existence of seven societal-level values and ten individual-level values across cultures. Although cultures may differ in terms of the degree to which specific values are endorsed, there appears to be a consistent structure to these values. Descriptions of the ten basic values pursued by individuals are listed below (Schwartz, 2011, p. 465).

- *Power*: Social status and prestige, control and dominance over people and resources.
- *Achievement*: Personal success through demonstrating competence according to social standards.
- *Hedonism*: Pleasure and sensuous gratification for oneself.
- *Stimulation*: Excitement, novelty, and challenge in life.
- *Self-direction*: Independent thought, and action – choosing, creating, exploring.
- *Universalism*: Understanding, appreciation, tolerance, and protection for the welfare of all people and for nature.
- *Benevolence*: Preservation and enhancement of the welfare of people with whom one is in frequent personal contact.
- *Tradition*: Respect, commitment, and acceptance of the customs and ideas that traditional culture or religion provide the self.
- *Conformity*: Restraint of actions, inclinations, and impulses likely to upset or harm others and violate social expectations or norms.
- *Security*: Safety, harmony, and stability of society, of relationships, and of self.

Which of these values were most evident in the products and behaviors you observed in the grocery store? Please provide examples of how these values were expressed.

Reference

Schwartz, S. H. (2011). Values: Individual and cultural. In F. J. R. van de Vijver, A. Chasiotis, & S. M. Breugelmans (Eds.), *Fundamental questions in cross-cultural psychology* (pp. 463–493). Cambridge, UK: Cambridge University Press.

ACTIVITY 7.3
VIRTUAL ETHNIC COMMUNITIES

Although in many countries there are neighborhoods or communities that are created by and cater to specific ethnic groups, technology now allows for the creation of ethnic-based communities online. Virtual communities may be especially important for ethnic groups that have been geographically dispersed. Naim Çınar (2016), who studied Turkish online communities in Norway, suggested that such sites aid immigrants' cultural learning and adaptation. This activity will explore the nature and functions of these communities.

Directions: Select a specific ethnic group as the focus of your investigation and then answer the questions below.

1. Describe the specific ethnic group you selected.

2. List and describe at least three to five websites that were created by the ethnic community you selected. Be sure to include the full web address (URL) of each.

3. List five to ten topics addressed on these sites.

4. Discuss some of the main functions served by virtual ethnic communities.

5. It is important to distinguish between sites created by the communities they serve and sites created (often by nonmembers) *about* those groups. Please describe some of the differences you observed between sites created by members and nonmembers of ethnic communities.

Thinking Further

1. Many more sites about women than men seem to have been created by people from outside of the ethnic community. Vernadette Gonzalez and Robyn Magalit Rodriguez (2003), for example, pointed out that a web search using the term *Filipino* (masculine form) yields information on national and cultural matters, whereas a web search using the term *Filipina* (feminine form) produces information on models, mail-order brides, and pornography. What gender differences did you find in the ethnic sites you investigated?

2. Jerry Kang (2003) raised an interesting question about race and ethnicity online: Are we more likely to achieve the conditions that favor prejudice reduction online than in person? The contact hypothesis (see Activity 8.10) states that prejudice is likely to be reduced when the contact involves people of equal status, is pleasant, is cooperative, allows people to get to know one another as individuals, and disconfirms stereotypes. Given these conditions, how would you assess the potential for prejudice reduction through encountering racial/ethnic differences online?

References

Çınar, N. (2016). Understanding the motives for joining ethnic online communities: A study of Turks in Norway. *Journal of Yasar University, 11*(42), 67–76.

Gonzalez, V. V., & Rodriguez, R. M. (2003). Filipina.com: Wives, workers, and whores on the cyberfrontier. In R. C. Lee & S. C. Wong (Eds.), *AsianAmerica. net: Ethnicity, nationalism, and cyberspace* (pp. 215–234). New York, NY: Routledge.

Kang, J. (2003). Cyber-race. In R. C. Lee & S. C. Wong (Eds.), *AsianAmerica.net: Ethnicity, nationalism, and cyberspace* (pp. 37–68). New York, NY: Routledge.

ACTIVITY 7.4
BARE BRANCHES

For the first time in human history, there is a massive gender imbalance in China and India with men outnumbering women by 70 million people (Denyer & Gowen, 2018). The young men in these countries are sometimes described as "bare branches," since they are unlikely to find a marriage partner and expand the family tree. This situation is a result of cultural preferences for boys coupled with the one child policy in China (from 1979–2016) and sex selection abortion and female infanticide in both countries. Scholars warn that this gender imbalance will have a significant effect beyond marriage rates in these countries and is likely to affect regional and global economies as well. This activity explores the implications of this situation through a consideration of gender roles across cultures.

Directions: Think about the roles, behaviors, and traits generally associated with men and women throughout the world. Then discuss the changes that might occur in a hypothetical society as a result of a disproportional number of men. Consider that, across cultures, gender stereotypes change along with changes in the behaviors of women and men (Miller, Eagly, & Linn, 2015). Some potential matters to consider are listed below:

- Age markers or milestones
- Care of elderly parents
- Crime rates
- Economic conditions
- Education
- Gender discrimination
- Gender roles
- Government policies
- Health and health care
- Home ownership
- Immigration and emigration
- Income inequality/social class
- Leisure activities
- Marriage and divorce rates and attitudes
- Mass media
- Mental illness
- Military service
- Occupations
- Personality traits
- Religion
- Sexual behavior
- Social class
- Status of women

Your description of a society where men outnumber women:

References

Denyer, S., & Gowen, A. (April 24, 2018). Too many men: China and India battle with the consequences of gender imbalance. *The Washington Post*.

Miller, D. I., Eagly, A. H., & Linn, M. C. (2015). Women's representation in science predicts national gender-science stereotypes: Evidence from 66 nations. *Journal of Educational Psychology, 107*(3), 631–644.

ACTIVITY 7.5
AGGRESSION ACROSS CULTURES: A QUIZ

This activity explores some of the factors that may help us to understand cross-cultural variation in aggressive behavior.

Directions: Decide whether each of the statements below is true or false. Then check your answers at the back of this book.

1. There are some societies that are free of aggression.   TRUE / FALSE

2. Across cultures, males are more physically and verbally aggressive than females   TRUE / FALSE

3. Exposure to violent video games is associated with aggression in Western societies but not in Eastern societies.   TRUE / FALSE

4. In cultures where aggression is repressed, it is ultimately expressed in destructive ways. TRUE / FALSE

5. The likelihood of warfare increases with the complexity of a society.   TRUE / FALSE

6. In the United States, one of the few industrialized nations practicing capital punishment, there is a negative correlation between the number of executions and the murder rate (that is, in areas where the rate of executions is high, the murder rate is low).   TRUE / FALSE

7. One of the best predictors of a country's homicide rate is the availability of firearms.   TRUE / FALSE

8. Across cultures studied, parental rejection is a strong predictor of children's violence.   TRUE / FALSE

9. People from the northern United States are more likely than people from the southern United States to react to insults with violence.   TRUE / FALSE

10. Studies across cultures find that most children who experience cyberbullying do not disclose experiences to their parents or other adults.   TRUE/FALSE

ACTIVITY 7.6
AN INTERCULTURAL CONFLICT

Over the past few decades there has been an increased effort to apply findings from cross-cultural research to the theory and practice of conflict resolution. Researchers have studied how cultural differences may impact perceptions of the process as well as the content of disputes. For example, Stella Ting-Toomey's face-negotiation theory addresses cultural differences in the *process* of conflict resolution (Ting-Toomey, 1988; Ting-Toomey & Oetzel, 2005). Her research indicated that members of individualistic cultures tend to use more direct methods of conflict management, whereas members of collectivistic cultures use more indirect methods of handling conflict. Ting-Toomey suggested that the less direct styles typically used by collectivists enable both parties to maintain face, defined as "an individual's claimed sense of favorable image in the context of social and relational networks" (Zhang, Ting-Toomey, & Oetzel, 2014, p. 373).

Bradford "J" Hall and Mutsumi Noguchi (1993) have addressed the *content* of intercultural disputes. These authors focus on the *kernel images* or key symbols involved in a dispute that may have varied meanings depending on the cultural context.

In this activity we will explore the role of cultural differences in both the content of a dispute and the process of conflict resolution in a simulation based on a case study documented by Hall and Noguchi (1993) and Ting-Toomey's model of conflict styles. The critical kernel image in this conflict is that of the dolphin.

Directions: Find two of your friends who are willing to act out a brief role play. After reading both parts yourself, assign one of your friends to the part of the Iki Fishermen's Representative and the other to the part of the Conservationists' Representative. Ask them to read the directions and then take part in a simulated negotiation based on the information they have been given. Be sure that the participants do not read each other's information sheets. Please take careful notes about the interaction so that you can more fully complete the questions at the end of this activity. Do not intervene in the simulated conflict negotiations unless the participants are at a standstill or are losing sight of the fact that this is only a simulation! (Your instructor can check the online *Instructor's Manual* that accompanies this book for information on the outcome of this actual dispute.)

Iki Fishermen's Representative

Directions: After you read the information below, you will be involved in a simulated negotiation with an individual playing the part of the Conservationists' Representative. Please do not change any of the facts of the case stated below. Feel free, however, to use your creativity to elaborate on these facts. You may introduce the information stated below into your negotiation as you see fit. Whenever possible, please use the negotiation style specified below.

Shared Background Information

- The crisis began when the arrival of a large number of dolphins in the waters surrounding the Japanese island of Iki was accompanied by a dramatic decrease in fishing output.
- In 1978, a report on Japanese TV documented the slaughter of over one thousand dolphins by the fishermen of Iki Island. The report was soon broadcast worldwide, resulting in shock and outrage in the West.
- Following the broadcast, several Western conservationists approached the Iki fishermen to discuss options for resolving the situation.
- The conservationists tried unsuccessfully to convince the fishermen that the dolphins were not responsible for the decrease in fishing output.
- When no agreement was initially reached, some conservationists took matters into their own hands, secretly freeing dolphins from the nets of the Iki fishermen.

Iki Fishermen's Perspective

- We are faced with a choice between standing by and losing our entire way of life or fighting to preserve our families, our community, and our livelihood.
- We were the ones who initially invited the Japanese reporters to cover the dolphin killings. We were trying to convey the gravity of our situation to our government so that they would provide assistance. However, our plea was intercepted by outsiders.
- The conservationists lack compassion and are incapable of understanding the plight of our people and the heroic battle we are waging.
- We view the *iruka* or dolphin as an evil creature, the gangster of the sea, the enemy of the fishermen.

- We use the term *iruka*, which means "sea pig" because, until the mid-1800s, dolphins were a primary source of protein for the Japanese people. Prior to that time, Buddhist tenets prohibited the consumption of four-legged animals.
- The dolphins killed at Iki were not eaten by people, but were used as fertilizer and pig food.
- In day-to-day discussion, we often substitute words such as *enemies, competitors, criminals*, or *gangsters* for the word *dolphin*.

Negotiation Style

- Directness and contradiction are avoided.
- Much of what is communicated is done so indirectly, through nuance, nonverbals, or in what is *not said*.
- Allowing members of the negotiation to maintain face or respect is critical.
- Expressions of respect and courtesy are important.
- The relationship between disputants must be mended if the conflict is to be resolved.
- Conflict typically involves violations of one's sense of group loyalty or ingroup/outgroup boundaries.
- It is important to recognize the historical roots of current conflicts.
- Silences are natural and useful.

J

Conservationists' Representative

Directions: After you read the information below, you will be involved in a simulated negotiation with an individual playing the part of the Iki Fishermen's Representative. Please do not change any of the facts of the case stated below. Feel free, however, to use your creativity to elaborate on these facts. You may introduce the information stated below into your negotiation as you see fit. Whenever possible, please use the negotiation style specified below.

Shared Background Information

- The crisis began when the arrival of a large number of dolphins in the waters surrounding the Japanese island of Iki was accompanied by a dramatic decrease in fishing output.
- In 1978, a report on Japanese TV documented the slaughter of over one thousand dolphins by the fishermen of Iki Island. The report was soon broadcast worldwide, resulting in shock and outrage in the West.
- Following the broadcast, several Western conservationists approached the Iki fishermen to discuss options for resolving the situation.
- The conservationists tried unsuccessfully to convince the fishermen that the dolphins were not responsible for the decrease in fishing output.
- When no agreement was initially reached, some conservationists took matters into their own hands, secretly freeing dolphins from the nets of the Iki fishermen.

Conservationists' Perspective

- We are concerned with the rights and freedom of all beings.
- The Japanese fishermen don't really understand the ecological situation. We have tried to make it clear to them that dolphins are not the cause of their declining catch.
- Concern with the lack of an agreement and the continued drift-net fishing on the part of the Japanese has led to heroic efforts by some of our side, risking their lives to free hundreds of dolphins under cover of darkness.
- Dolphins are endangered.
- Dolphins are highly intelligent and friendly animals that have a special bond with humans.
- The Western image of dolphins has its roots in Greek mythology in which the special status of dolphins allowed them to communicate with the Gods.
- The concept of killing, and particularly eating, dolphins is repulsive to us.

Negotiation Style

- Directness and confrontation are admirable.
- Conflict is dysfunctional if it is suppressed.
- The relationship between individuals involved in a dispute should be separate from "the issues."
- Conflict typically involves violations of one's sense of power, autonomy, or fairness.
- It is important to justify one's position and build up credibility.
- Bringing up the historical roots of current conflicts is generally a waste of time.
- Silences are uncomfortable.

1. How did the participants react to the differences in negotiation style?

2. How did differences in "kernel image" enter into this dispute?

3. Were the participants able to negotiate a resolution? If so, what strategies were helpful in coming to agreement? If not, what obstacles impeded the resolution of this dispute?

4. Were cultural differences in content or process directly discussed by the participants? If so, how was this accomplished? If not, do you think making the cultural differences explicit would have been helpful?

Thinking Further

Do you think a third party (mediator) might have facilitated the resolution of this dispute? Please explain.

Source

Simulation adapted from Hall, B. J., & Noguchi, M. Intercultural conflict: A case study. *International Journal of Intercultural Relations, 17*, 399–413. Copyright © 1993 by Elsevier Science. Adapted with permission.

References

Hall, B. J., & Noguchi, M. (1993). Intercultural conflict: A case study. *International Journal of Intercultural Relations, 17*, 399–413.

Ting-Toomey, S. (1988). Intercultural conflict styles: A face-negotiation theory. In Y. Y. Kim & W. GudyKunst (Eds.), *Theories in intercultural communication* (pp. 213–235). Newbury Park, CA: Sage.

Ting-Toomey, S., & Oetzel, J. G. (2005). The matrix of face: An updated face-negotiation theory. In W. B. Gudykunst (Ed)., *Theorizing about intercultural communication* (pp. 71–92). Thousand Oaks, CA: Sage.

Zhang, Q., Ting-Toomey, S., & Oetzel, J. G. (2014). Linking emotion to the conflict face-negotiation theory: A U.S.–China investigation of the mediating effects of anger, compassion, and guilt in interpersonal conflict. *Human Communication Research, 40*(3), 373–395.

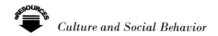

ACTIVITY 7.7
WORK-RELATED VALUES

The basis of much cross-cultural research in – and outside of – the workplace is Geert Hofstede's (1980; 2001) research on work-related values. Hofstede studied the values of IBM employees in over 70 countries. Based on this data he derived four dimensions of cultural variability: *individualism-collectivism, power distance, uncertainty avoidance*, and *masculinity-femininity*. Hofstede used the average scores of workers in each country to rank countries on the four dimensions. Several years later, the Chinese Culture Connection (1987), a group of researchers led by Michael Harris Bond, identified the value Confucian Work Dynamism. Hofstede added this dimension to his model, which he labeled *long- versus short-term orientation* (Hofstede, 2001). Finally, a sixth dimension, *indulgence-restraint*, was added based on Michael Minkov's analysis of World Values Survey data (Hofstede, Hofstede, & Minkov, 2010). The purpose of this activity is to better understand these six dimensions by applying them to a workplace with which you are familiar.

Directions: First write a brief description of a work setting with which you are familiar. Then read the descriptions of the six dimensions below and in the questions that follow apply these dimensions to your work setting.

Workplace Description (include type of business or occupation, approximate number of employees, and structure in terms of managers and subordinates):

Work-related Values

As compared to individualistic cultures, cultures high in collectivism tend to be characterized by:

- A focus on the goals of the group rather than individual goals
- Achievement attributed to the efforts of the group rather than the individual
- Avoidance of confrontation
- The perception that direct requests are an ineffective form of communication
- Working in groups

Cultures high in power distance tend to be characterized by:

- Clear distinctions between superiors and subordinates
- The acceptance of an unequal power distribution
- Dependence of subordinates on superiors
- Conformity
- Unquestioning compliance with the orders of superiors

Cultures high in uncertainty avoidance tend to be characterized by:

- Lower tolerance for ambiguity
- Greater need for consensus
- Greater need for formal rules
- Avoidance of conflict
- Resistance to change

As compared to feminine cultures, cultures high in masculinity are characterized by:

- A high value on things as opposed to people
- A focus on power and competition as opposed to nurturance
- The perception that work is central to one's life
- An emphasis on distinct gender roles

As compared to cultures with short-term orientation, those with long-term orientation tend to be characterized by:

- Patience and perseverance
- Thrift

- Organizations modeled after the structure of the family
- Having a sense of shame

As compared to those high in indulgence, cultures high in restraint tend to be characterized by:

- A focus on controlling impulses
- A value on maintaining order
- Low importance of leisure
- Little sense of personal control in life
- Pessimism

1. Is this workplace more individualist or collectivist? Please explain.

2. Does this workplace have high, moderate, or low power distance? Please explain.

3. Does this workplace have high, moderate, or low uncertainty avoidance? Please explain.

4. Is this workplace more feminine or masculine? Please explain.

5. Does this workplace have more of a long-term or short-term orientation? Please explain.

6. Does this workplace have more indulgence or restraint? Please explain.

Thinking Further

Are the values manifested in this workplace conducive to a diverse workforce? Please explain.

References

Chinese Culture Connection. (1987). Chinese values and the search for culture-free dimensions of culture. *Journal of Cross-Cultural Psychology, 18*, 143–164.

Hofstede, G. (1980). *Culture's consequences: International differences in work-related values*. Newbury Park, CA: Sage.

Hofstede, G. (2001). *Culture's consequences: Comparing values, behaviors, and organizations across nations* (2nd ed.). Beverly Hills, CA: Sage.

Hofstede, G., Hofstede, G. J., & Minkov, M. (2010). *Cultures and organizations: Software of the mind* (3rd ed.). New York, NY: McGraw-Hill.

ACTIVITY 7.8
LEADERSHIP STYLES

A major interest of those who study organizational behavior is how to select and train effective leaders. Leadership becomes an even greater concern when it involves international businesses or organizations within a country that have a diverse workforce. This activity explores universality and cultural variability in the concept of leadership.

Directions: Spend a few minutes thinking about your image of a leader. Then complete the five sentences below to describe characteristics of a good leader and answer the questions that follow.

- A good leader _____
- A good leader _____
- A good leader _____
- A good leader _____
- A good leader _____

1. Do you think that the characteristics you described above are universal across cultures or culture-specific? Please explain.

2. Project GLOBE is an extensive multi-stage study of leadership behavior across cultures for which questionnaire, interview, and observational data were collected in 62 countries in 2004 (House, Hanges, Javidan, Dorfman, & Gupta, 2004) and 24 countries in 2014 (House, Dorfman, Mansour, Hanges, & de Luque, 2014). One goal of Project GLOBE researchers is to identify universal attributes of effective leaders and to determine how leadership varies across cultures. These researchers found that across cultures, leaders with charismatic behavior (they are encouraging, positive, motivational, and confidence builders) and team-oriented behavior (they build consensus and focus on collaborative problem solving) have the most impact on the company's performance.

    Discuss how these findings compare with the characteristics of good leaders you listed above.

3. What basic human needs might be reflected in these universal preferences for leaders with charisma and team-oriented behavior?

Thinking Further

1. Project GLOBE also identified several cultural differences in leadership style. For example, the Southern Asia Cluster (India, Indonesia, Philippines, Malaysia, Thailand, and Iran) is characterized by leadership that is family-oriented (Gupta, Hanges, & Dorfman, 2002). Jai B. P. Sinha (1995), for example, described the Indian manager as a nurturant task leader who acts toward the employees as a parent would toward a child. Treating each subordinate fairly, then, does not mean treating them all the same, but making sure that the needs of each are met to the extent possible. As these needs differ, so will the treatment. According to Sinha, leadership in the businesses of India involves more participation in the projects of subordinates rather than merely giving instructions as to which tasks are to be undertaken. Furthermore, there is not the distinction between work and personal life that one finds in much of the Western world. The manager is expected to provide advice and at times intervene if an employee is experiencing problems unrelated to work. For example, a manager in India may suggest a marriage partner for an employee or provide guidance in family disputes.

   Would a person having the five characteristics you listed at the beginning of this activity make an effective leader in the Indian context Sinha describes? If not, what other characteristics would be important?

2. Sekhar (2001) noted that leadership in India varies a great deal from region to region. What factors do you think might influence such regional differences within countries?

3. Based on Project GLOBE data, Amanda Bullough and Mary Sully de Luque (2015) investigated the environments that are conducive for women to participate in as business and political leaders. Their results indicated that in settings where a charismatic leadership style is valued (emphasizing encouraging and motivating others), women are more likely to participate in both political and business leadership roles. However, women are less likely to participate in leadership roles, particularly in political positions, when a self-protective leadership style is valued (emphasizing competition and status).

What might this mean for the participation of women in business and political leadership in your country?

4. Recent studies (e.g., Lisak & Erez, 2015; Maldonado & Vera, 2014; Rosenauer, Homan, Horstmeier, & Voelpel, 2016) point to cultural intelligence as an important characteristic of competent leaders. Describe below any additional characteristics of a good leader that would facilitate cultural intelligence.

References

Bullough, A., & de Luque, M. S. (2015). Women's participation in entrepreneurial and political leadership: The importance of culturally endorsed implicit leadership theories. *Leadership, 11*(1), 36–56.

Gupta, V., Hanges, P. J., & Dorfman, P. (2002). Cultural clusters: Methodology and findings. *Journal of World Business, 37*, 11–15.

House, R. J., Hanges, P. J., Javidan, M., Dorfman, P. W., & Gupta, V. (Eds.). (2004). *Culture, leadership, and organizations: The GLOBE study of 62 societies*. Thousand Oaks, CA: Sage.

House, R. J., Dorfman, P. W., Mansour, J., Hanges, P. J., & de Luque, M. S. (2014). *Strategic leadership across cultures: GLOBE Study of CEO leadership behavior and effectiveness in 24 countries*. Thousand Oaks, CA: Sage.

Lisak, A., & Erez, M. (2015). Leadership emergence in multicultural teams: The power of global characteristics. *Journal of World Business, 50*(1), 3–14.

Maldonado, T., & Vera, D. (2014). Leadership skills for international crises: The role of cultural intelligence and improvisation. *Organizational Dynamics, 43*(4), 257–265.

Rosenauer, D., Homan, A. C., Horstmeier, C. A. L., & Voelpel, S. C. (2016). Managing nationality diversity: The interactive effect of leaders' cultural intelligence and task interdependence. *British Journal of Management, 27*(3), 628–645.

Sekhar, R. C. (2001). Trends in ethics and styles of leadership in India. *Business Ethics: A European Review, 10*, 360–363.

Sinha, J. B. P. (1995). *The Cultural Context of Leadership and Power*. New Delhi: Sage.

ACTIVITY 7.9
CHOOSING A MATE

Starting in the late 1980s, David Buss (Buss et al., 1990) and other evolutionary psychologists conducted a number of cross-cultural studies to identify the characteristics women and men prefer in a long-term partner. This activity will familiarize you with some of the major findings of this research and allow you to compare your own mate selection preferences with these research findings.

Directions: Complete the items below using the five-point scale to indicate the importance you place on each characteristic in choosing a life partner, then answer the questions that follow.

Very Unimportant				Very Important
1	2	3	4	5

1. Kind and understanding   1 2 3 4 5

2. Family has good reputation   1 2 3 4 5

3. Similar religious beliefs   1 2 3 4 5

4. Exciting personality   1 2 3 4 5

5. Creative and artistic   1 2 3 4 5

6. Good housekeeper   1 2 3 4 5

7. Intelligent   1 2 3 4 5

8. Good earning capacity   1 2 3 4 5

9. Wants children   1 2 3 4 5

10. Easygoing   1 2 3 4 5

11. College graduate   1 2 3 4 5

12. Someone my family approves of 1 2 3 4 5

13. Physically attractive   1 2 3 4 5

14. Healthy   1 2 3 4 5

15. Love   1 2 3 4 5

1. Circle the characteristics you rated as most important (4 or 5). What might be the reason why you selected these particular items?

2. Todd Shackelford, David Schmitt, and David Buss (2005) analyzed data on mate preferences from 37 cultures located on six continents and five islands. Their findings were representative of previous studies in that men were more likely to value physical attractiveness and women were more likely to value a high earning potential. How do your responses compare with these findings?

3. Evolutionary psychologists, such as Shackelford, Schmitt, and Buss have argued that when looking for a long-term partner, men will value physical attractiveness because it is a cue to their partner's fertility whereas women value economic security to provide for her and her children during the extended period of child care after birth. An alternative explanation comes from biosocial theory (Wood & Eagly, 2002), which suggests that sex differences in mate preference reflect a need to adopt traits and preferences that will be most helpful given the physical attributes of men and women as well as the gender roles that arise from a specific social and ecological context. This latter approach is supported by the finding that the sex differences in mate preferences appear to be decreasing with greater gender equality (Bech-Sørensen, & Pollet, 2016).

   Do the characteristics that you rated as most important to you best fit an evolutionary perspective or a biosocial perspective? Please explain.

Thinking Further

1. Studies show that love is viewed as an important basis for mate selection world-wide, although slightly more so in countries with greater wealth (Sprecher & Hatfield, 2017). Why might that be the case?

2. Although there appears to be a global trend away from formal arranged marriages (Dion & Dion, 2005), in many cultures throughout the world, families play a major part in mate selection, often identifying potential partners who will be a good fit with the family's needs and standards (Buunk, Park, & Duncan, 2010). What is the role of your family in your mate selection? What advantages might there be to family input into this process?

3. You may be surprised to learn that media plays a significant role in perceptions of future mates across cultures (Chen & Austin, 2017). In what ways, if any, has the media influenced your preferences for a mate?

4. Cross-cultural research on mate preferences has focused primarily on hetero-sexual couples. What might be some reasons why there is so little research on mate preferences among same sex couples? How might this be remedied?

Source

Items adapted from Shackelford, T. K., Schmitt, D. P., & Buss, D. M. Universal dimensions of human mate preferences. *Personality and Individual Differences, 39*(2), 447–458. Copyright © 2005 by Elsevier. Adapted with permission.

References

Bech-Sørensen, J., & Pollet, T. V. (2016). Sex differences in mate preferences: A replication study, 20 years later. *Evolutionary Psychological Science, 2*, 71–176.

Buss, D. M., Abbott, M., Angleitner, A., Asherian, A., Biaggio, A., Blanco-Villasenor, A., et. al. (1990). International preferences in selecting mates: A study of 37 cultures. *Journal of Cross-Cultural Psychology, 21*, 5–47.

Buunk, A. P., Park, J. H., & Duncan, L. A. (2010). Cultural variation in parental influence on mate choice. *Cross-Cultural Research: The Journal of Comparative Social Science, 44*(1), 23–40.

Chen, R., & Austin, J. P. (2017). The effect of external influences on mate selection necessity traits: Cross-cultural comparisons of Chinese and American men and women. *Marriage & Family Review, 53*(3), 246–261.

Dion, K. L., & Dion, K. K. (2005). Culture and relationships: The downside of self-contained individualism. In R. M. Sorrentino, D. Cohen, J. M. Olson, & M. P. Zanna (Eds.), *Cultural and social behavior: The Ontario Symposium* (Vol. 10, pp. 77–94). Mahwah, NJ: Erlbaum,

Shackelford, T. K., Schmitt, D. P., & Buss, D. M. (2005). Universal dimensions of human mate preferences. *Personality and Individual Differences, 39*(2), 447–458.

Sprecher, S., & Hatfield, E. (2017). The importance of love as a basis of marriage: Revisiting Kephart (1967). *Journal of Family Issues, 38*, 312–335.

Wood, W., & Eagly, A. H. (2002). A cross-cultural analysis of the behavior of women and men: Implications for the origins of sex differences. *Psychological Bulletin, 128*(5), 699–727.

ACTIVITY 7.10
INTERCULTURAL PARTNERSHIPS

The frequency of intercultural romantic partnerships is increasing rapidly in many parts of the world. Early writing on intercultural relationships focused on pathological motivation for entering into these unions, such as rebelling against one's own culture or even unconscious hatred of one's opposite sex parent (and thus choosing a partner who does not physically resemble him or her!). We now know that most people enter intercultural relationships for the same reasons most people enter intracultural (same culture) relationships: warmth, love, affection, excitement, caring, intimacy, and solidarity (Jeter, 1982). In fact, people in enduring intercultural partnerships may even have or develop some special skills for dealing with cultural differences (Tili & Barker, 2015). This activity will allow you to explore some of the challenges and adaptations of people in intercultural relationships.

Directions: For this activity you are to interview someone who is involved in an intercultural dating relationship, marriage, or committed partnership.

Select a respondent. It is up to you to determine what constitutes "intercultural" here. Researchers of intercultural relationships have focused primarily on individuals who differ in terms of race/ethnicity, religion, and nationality. For this activity, however, you may define intercultural more broadly.

Check for time constraints. Reserve at least 15 minutes for the interview.

Obtain informed consent. Explain the purpose of the interview (to explore the challenges of intercultural partnerships) and be sure that your respondent understands that his or her responses may be discussed in class or included in a written report.

Assure and maintain confidentiality. Be sure you tell your respondent that you will not in any way attach his or her name to the responses in reporting or discussing the responses to the interview. It is critical that you maintain this confidentiality in order to conduct the interview in an ethical manner.

Conduct the interview. Ask the interview questions in the order in which they appear in this activity. Be sure to take notes in the space provided or on a separate sheet.

Provide feedback to the respondent if appropriate. If you have some general conclusions about intercultural relationships based on discussing or analyzing the interview data with your class, you might convey these conclusions to your respondents. Be sure to thank him or her for the time they spent assisting you with this exercise.

Interview Questions

1. In what way is your relationship with your partner an intercultural relationship? Please explain.

2. Please describe one or two cultural differences that have affected your relationship with your partner.

3. Please describe the most useful strategy you have used in dealing with cultural differences in your relationship.

4. Please describe the least useful strategy you have used in dealing with cultural differences in your relationship.

5. As a couple, do you spend more time with individuals from your own cultural background, from your partner's cultural background, both, or neither? Please explain how this has affected your relationship.

6. Have you learned any skills, as a result of being in an intercultural relationship, that would assist you in other types of intercultural situations?

Analysis

1. The list below is adapted from Dugan Romano's (2001) work on common challenges for intercultural couples. Circle any of these challenges that seem to characterize the relationship of your interviewee.

   a. values
   b. food and drink
   c. politics
   d. gender roles
   e. time
   f. place of residence

   g. friends
   h. finances
   i. partner's family
   j. social class
   k. religion
   l. raising children

   m. response to stress
   n. conflict-handling style
   o. response to illness
   p. sexual behavior
   q. communication or language

   Please explain how your interviewee has faced the challenges you indicated.

2. Romano (2001) described four types of relationships she identified in research on intercultural marriages, labeled Submission/Immersion, Obliteration, Compromise, and Consensus. After reading the explanations of each of these types, decide which best fits the circumstances of your interviewee.

   - *Submission/Immersion*: One partner virtually abandons his or her own culture while immersing him- or herself in the culture of the other partner.
   - *Obliteration*: The couple forms a new third culture identity, maintaining none of the practices of their original cultures and thus eliminating all cultural differences.
   - *Compromise*: Each partner gives up some (often important) aspects of his or her own culture to allow for the other's cultural practices or beliefs.

- *Consensus*: The couple makes an ongoing search for solutions in which neither partner sacrifices aspects of culture essential to his or her well-being. Partners allow each other to be different without viewing difference as threatening.

Which (if any) of the four types above best characterizes the relationship of your interviewee? Please explain.

3. Discuss what you have learned from this interview about effective and ineffective strategies for intercultural interaction.

Thinking Further

1. Put an "X" in the blank to indicate which of the following relationships you would consider to be intercultural (assume each difference stated below is the only major difference between partners).

_____ a. One partner is Swiss; the other is Chilean.

_____ b. One partner is Buddhist; the other is Christian.

_____ c. One partner is wealthy; the other is middle class.

_____ d. One partner is deaf; the other is hearing.

_____ e. One partner is a first generation Korean immigrant; the other is a third generation Korean immigrant.

_____ f. One partner comes from a rural area; the other partner comes from an urban area (of the same country).

_____ g. One partner is male; the other is female.

---

2. Based on the items that you indicated above and on your interview data, write a definition of intercultural partnership.

References

Jeter, K. (1982). Analytic essay: Intercultural and interracial marriage. *Marriage and Family Review*, *5*, 105–111.

Romano, D. (2001). *Intercultural marriage: Promises and pitfalls* (2nd. ed.). Boston, MA: Nicholas Brealey.

Tili, T. R., & Barker, G. G. (2015). Communication in intercultural marriages: Managing cultural differences and conflicts. *Southern Communication Journal*, *80*(3), 189–210.

Intergroup Relations

ACTIVITY 8.1
DISCRIMINATION INCIDENTS

Discrimination has been defined as "treating people differently from others based primarily on membership in a social group" (Kite & Whitley, 2016, p. 16). A large number of psychological studies have focused on the characteristics of people who engage in discriminatory behavior and their cognitive processes. In recent decades, however, there has been increased attention to how one experiences discriminatory behavior (e.g., Alvarez, Liang, & Neville, 2016) as well as to causes of discrimination beyond the individual (e.g., Offermann et al., 2014). This activity is designed to encourage you to think about what constitutes discrimination, why it occurs, and the effects on the target of discrimination.

Directions: In the space provided below, please write an account of an incident of discrimination that you experienced, witnessed, or otherwise learned about. Then answer the questions on the following pages.

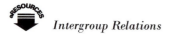

1. Which of the following likely led to this incident of discrimination?

- *Interpersonal* factors, such as an individuals' attitudes or beliefs
- *Institutional* factors, such as the policies or practices of an organization (e.g., a business, school, or government) that systematically favors some group(s) of people over others
- *Cultural* factors, such as widely held stereotypes or messages about values that are disseminated through popular culture and mass media

Please explain.

2. Who is privileged by this form of discrimination?

3. What were (or might be) the short- and long-term effects of this incident on the target of the discrimination?

4. How could this form of discrimination be prevented?

References

Alvarez, A. N., Liang, C. T. H., & Neville, H. A. (Eds.). (2016). *The cost of racism for people of color: Contextualizing experiences of discrimination.* Washington, DC: American Psychological Association.

Kite, M. E., & Whitley, B. E. (2016). *The psychology of prejudice and discrimination* (3rd ed.). Belmont, CA: Wadsworth.

Offermann, L. R., Basford, T. E., Graebner, R., Jaffer, S., De Graaf, S. B., & Kaminsky, S. E. (2014). See no evil: Color blindness and perceptions of subtle racial discrimination in the workplace. *Cultural Diversity and Ethnic Minority Psychology, 20*(4), 499–507.

ACTIVITY 8.2
EXPLORING PRIVILEGE

Although most of us readily acknowledge the discrimination that exists in our societies, we often have difficulty recognizing the forms of unearned privilege that are the counterpart of discrimination. For example, imagine that a White woman and a Black woman walk into a clothing store at the same time. There are several unoccupied salespeople in the store. One salesperson rushes to assist the White customer. No one assists the Black customer. We can easily understand that the Black customer is the target of discrimination. What may be more difficult to understand is that the White customer is the recipient of an unearned privilege. This activity will help you explore this concept of privilege and understand how you as an individual may or may not be privileged.

Directions: For each of the categories below, read the example and write a second example of the form of privilege specified.

1. White skin privilege: [Example: I can be pretty sure that hiring decisions will be based on my skills and experience.]

2. Male privilege: [Example: I can travel on my own with little fear of being harassed.]

3. Heterosexual privilege: [Example: I can freely introduce my significant other to family or coworkers.]

4. Able-bodied privilege: [Example: I can make plans without having to check whether transportation, parking, buildings, seating, or restrooms are accessible.]

5. Middle class privilege: [Example: If I become ill, I can be confident that I will receive the medical treatment I need.]

6. What other forms of privilege exist? Identify one additional form of privilege and write a statement illustrating that form of privilege below.

Thinking Further

1. Most people have not given much thought to the forms of privilege they experience. Why do you think we are relatively unaware of the privileges we receive?

2. Do you think that once we are aware of one form of privilege we are better able to understand other forms of privilege? Why or why not?

3. How can people become more aware of the ways in which they are privileged?

ACTIVITY 8.3
INSTITUTIONAL DISCRIMINATION

The term *institutional racism* was first introduced by Stokely Carmichael and Charles V. Hamilton in their 1967 book, *Black Power*. They used this term to distinguish between the racist behavior of *individuals* and the policies and practices of *institutions* that perpetuate racism. Institutional discrimination is not limited to issues of race but includes the systematic perpetuation of other forms of inequality as well. This activity explores the concept of institutional discrimination; that is, policies or practices of organizations that *systematically* privilege members of some groups and discriminate against members of other groups.

Directions: For each of the policies below, determine whether it is a form of institutional discrimination. If you find it is, then please answer the additional questions following each policy.

1. In many states in the U.S., people are required to show a government issued identification card in order to vote. Obtaining this card may require waiting in line at a department of motor vehicles or other government office, presenting proof of residency and a form of identification such as a birth certificate, and often paying a fee.

   a. This is institutional discrimination: Yes _____ No _____

   b. Against which groups, if any, might this policy discriminate?

   c. What is the purpose of this policy?

   d. If this purpose is a valid one, how else might it be achieved?

2. Children of alumni receive preference for admission into some colleges and universities.

   a. This is institutional discrimination: Yes _____ No _____

   b. Against which groups, if any, might this policy discriminate?

---

c. What is the purpose of this policy?

d. If this purpose is a valid one, how else might it be achieved?

3. As part of their marketing strategy, some retail companies seek people with a specific "look" to staff their stores.

   a. This is institutional discrimination: Yes _____ No _____

   b. Against which groups, if any, might this policy discriminate?

   c. What is the purpose of this policy?

   d. If this purpose is a valid one, how else might it be achieved?

4. In several countries, persons accused of a crime who cannot post bail remain in prison while awaiting trial.

   a. This is institutional discrimination: Yes _____ No _____

   b. Against which groups, if any, might this policy discriminate?

   c. What is the purpose of this policy?

   d. If this purpose is a valid one, how else might it be achieved?

5. Many corporations fill position openings "in-house" rather than advertise.

   a. This is institutional discrimination: Yes _____ No _____

   b. Against which groups, if any, might this policy discriminate?

   c. What is the purpose of this policy?

   d. If this purpose is a valid one, how else might it be achieved?

6. White actors are frequently chosen to play the part of People of Color.

   a. This is institutional discrimination: Yes _____ No _____

   b. Against which groups, if any, might this policy discriminate?

   c. What is the purpose of this policy?

   d. If this purpose is a valid one, how else might it be achieved?

Reference

Carmichael, S., & Hamilton, C. V. (1967). *Black power: The politics of liberation in America*. New York, NY: Vintage Books.

ACTIVITY 8.4
GEOGRAPHIC KNOWLEDGE AND
INTERGROUP ATTITUDES

Several studies have found a link between geographical knowledge and attitudes about countries other than one's own. For example, a study conducted by Kyle Dropp for the *New York Times* found that U.S. Americans were more likely to support a diplomatic solution to conflicts with North Korea over military action if they could find North Korea on a map (only 36% could; Quealy, 2017). Fabio Lorenzi-Cioldi and colleagues had participants from Belgium, Ivory Coast, Italy, Kosovo, Portugal, and Switzerland draw the borders between their own and neighboring countries on boundary-free maps. They found that in general the tendency to underestimate the size of another country was associated with more negative attitudes toward that country (Lorenzi-Cioldi, Chatard, Marques, Selimbegovic, Konan, & Faniko, 2011).

Directions: For this activity you will do your own informal test of a connection between geographic knowledge and intergroup attitudes. First, identify a current issue involving the relationship between your own and another country. Then write two questions to gauge attitudes about the issue and those involved. Finally, find an outline map – one that shows borders without labeling the countries (there are many available for classroom use online). Ask ten people to respond to your questions and to identify the country you have chosen on your outline map. Be sure to write down their responses and to use a clean copy of the outline map for each participant so that they won't be influenced by each other's responses. Examples below are based on the methods used in the studies conducted by Dropp and by Lorenzi-Cioldi and colleagues.

1. Briefly describe the issue and countries involved that you have chosen as your focus (for example, tensions between the U.S. and North Korea following a series of long-range missile tests by North Korea and an exchange of threats between the North Korean leader and the U.S. President.)

2. Below, list the questions you developed to assess intergroup attitudes (for example, "Do you think the U.S. should conduct airstrikes against North Korea?" and "Agree or disagree – most North Koreans are good people).

3. Paste your outline map and instructions below (for example, "Make a mark on the map below to indicate the location of North Korea").

Did you find any relationship between the participants' ability to identify the country on a map and their answers to the two questions? (Note that this was an informal rather than scientific study, so we can't be certain that other factors did not influence the responses.) Please discuss your findings below.

Thinking Further

1. How might we explain any relationship between attitudes about a country and the ability to locate it on a map?

2. In Dropp's study, those who could find North Korea on a map tended to be more educated, older (perhaps alive during the Korean War), know someone of Korean ancestry, or have traveled internationally. What factors might predict geographical knowledge in your survey?

3. Surveys conducted by the National Geographic Society show great variations in geographic literacy across countries, with students in the U.S. scoring particularly poorly (e.g., Council on Foreign Relations/National Geographic Society, 2016). Other than differences in school curricula, such as requirements for geography course work, what might contribute to these differences in geographic literacy?

4. What are some ideas for improving geographic literacy in young people today?

References

Council on Foreign Relations/National Geographic Society. (2016). *What college-aged students know about the world: A survey on global literacy.* Washington, DC: Author.

Lorenzi-Cioldi, F., Chatard, A., Marques, J. M., Selimbegovic, L., Konan, P., & Faniko, K. (2011). What do drawings reveal about people's attitudes towards countries and their citizens? *Social Psychology, 42*(3), 231–240.

Quealy, K. (July 5, 2017). If Americans can find North Korea on a map, they're more likely to prefer diplomacy. *New York Times.*

ACTIVITY 8.5
INTERNALIZED OPPRESSION

One possible consequence of being the target of discrimination is *internalized oppression*. This occurs when people come to view and treat themselves and other members of their group in the same ways that they have been stereotyped or mistreated as targets. Although internalized oppression does not always happen on a conscious level it can have serious physical and mental health consequences (David & Derthick, 2014). For example, internalized racism is associated with glucose intolerance (a precursor to diabetes) among Afro-Caribbean women (Butler, Tull, Chambers, & Taylor, 2002) and among LGBTQ individuals, internalized oppression is a predictor of problems with substance abuse (Drazdowski et al., 2016). The aim of this activity is to explore the concept of internalized oppression.

Directions: Read the following list of behaviors and decide for each whether it indicates internalized oppression. Please explain your answer in the space provided.

1. Passing as a member of an ethnic/racial group other than one's own.

2. Using solutions or creams to lighten one's skin color.

3. Telling jokes about one's own ethnic group or sexual identity.

---

4. Undergoing surgery to alter facial features associated with one's ethnic/racial group.

5. Striving to eliminate one's accent from a working-class community in favor of a more middle- or upper-class manner of speaking.

References

Butler, C., Tull, E. S., Chambers, E. C., & Taylor, J. (2002). Internalized racism, body fat distribution, and abnormal fasting glucose among African-Caribbean women in Dominica, West Indies. *Journal of the National Medical Association, 94*, 143–148.

David, E. J. R., & Derthick, A. O. (2014). What is internalized oppression, and so what? In E. J. R. David (Ed.), *Internalized oppression: The psychology of marginalized groups* (pp. 31–56). New York, NY: Springer.

Drazdowski, T. K., Perrin, P. B., Trujillo, M., Sutter, M., Benotsch, E. G., & Snipes, D. J. (2016). Structural equation modeling of the effects of racism, LGBTQ discrimination, and internalized oppression on illicit drug use in LGBTQ people of color. *Drug and Alcohol Dependence, 159*, 255–262.

ACTIVITY 8.6
COGNITION AND STEREOTYPE FORMATION

Research in cognitive psychology indicates that stereotyping is in part a result of the way humans process information (see, for example, Hinton, 2016). The way we categorize, memorize and explain events is generally adaptive, but under some circumstances can lead us to develop and maintain stereotypes. This activity will demonstrate some of the cognitive processes involved in stereotyping.

Directions: You will need to request the assistance of four volunteers for this activity. Each of the participants will listen to a slightly different description. Read the descriptions below to the participant indicated. The participant should then complete the appropriate questionnaire. You will note that the descriptions vary in terms of the age and gender of the stimulus person. Once you have collected responses from all four participants, answer the questions on the pages that follow.

Read to Participant A: We are asking for volunteers as part of a class project on the processes involved in forming mental imagery. Please listen to the following description and focus on the images that form in response. You will then be asked to complete a brief questionnaire.

Sara is 27 years old. She is taking courses at her local community college and working part-time. A few years ago, she moved from a more urban area to an apartment complex in the suburbs. She lives alone, except for a pet. She is in good health and tries to get some exercise several times a week. She has made friends with one of her neighbors with whom she occasionally cooks a meal. She has several hobbies and enjoys the outdoors.

Read to Participant B: We are asking for volunteers as part of a class project on the processes involved in forming mental imagery. Please listen to the following description and focus on the images that form in response. You will then be asked to complete a brief questionnaire.

Sara is 67 years old. She is taking courses at her local community college and working part-time. A few years ago, she moved from a more urban area to an apartment complex in the suburbs. She lives alone, except for a pet. She is in good health and tries to get some exercise several times a week. She has made friends with one of her neighbors with whom she occasionally cooks a meal. She has several hobbies and enjoys the outdoors.

Read to Participant C: We are asking for volunteers as part of a class project on the processes involved in forming mental imagery. Please listen to the following description and focus on the images that form in response. You will then be asked to complete a brief questionnaire.

Sam is 27 years old. He is taking courses at his local community college and working part-time. A few years ago, he moved from a more urban area to an apartment complex in the suburbs. He lives alone, except for a pet. He is in good health and tries to get some exercise several times a week. He has made friends with one of his neighbors with whom he occasionally cooks a meal. He has several hobbies and enjoys the outdoors.

Read to Participant D: We are asking for volunteers as part of a class project on the processes involved in forming mental imagery. Please listen to the following description and focus on the images that form in response. You will then be asked to complete a brief questionnaire.

Sam is 67 years old. He is taking courses at his local community college and working part-time. A few years ago, he moved from a more urban area to an apartment complex in the suburbs. He lives alone, except for a pet. He is in good health and tries to get some exercise several times a week. He has made friends with one of his neighbors with whom he occasionally cooks a meal. He has several hobbies and enjoys the outdoors.

Participant A

Please think about the person who was just described to you for a moment. In the space below, write down everything you can remember about this person. When you have finished writing down what you remember, please answer the questions on the next page.

Based on your image of Sara, please answer the following questions. If you do not have enough information to answer a particular question, draw on your image of Sara to answer as best you can.

1. How old is Sara?

2. What kind of courses was Sara taking?

3. What kind of work did Sara do?

4. Why did Sara move to the suburbs?

5. What kind of pet did she have?

6. How is her health?

7. What kind of exercise does she do?

8. Why does she occasionally cook with her neighbor?

9. What do you think she cooks?

10. What are her hobbies?

11. What does she enjoy doing outdoors?

12. Do you think Sara is someone you would enjoy meeting? Why or why not?

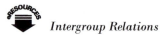

Participant B

Please think about the person who was just described to you for a moment. In the space below, write down everything you can remember about this person. When you have finished writing down what you remember, please answer the questions on the next page.

Based on your image of Sara, please answer the following questions. If you do not have enough information to answer a particular question, draw on your image of Sara to answer as best you can.

1. How old is Sara?

2. What kind of courses was Sara taking?

3. What kind of work did Sara do?

4. Why did Sara move to the suburbs?

5. What kind of pet did she have?

6. How is her health?

7. What kind of exercise does she do?

8. Why does she occasionally cook with her neighbor?

9. What do you think she cooks?

10. What are her hobbies?

11. What does she enjoy doing outdoors?

12. Do you think Sara is someone you would enjoy meeting? Why or why not?

Participant C

Please think about the person who was just described to you for a moment. In the space below, write down everything you can remember about this person. When you have finished writing down what you remember, please answer the questions on the next page.

Based on your image of Sam, please answer the following questions. If you do not have enough information to answer a particular question, draw on your image of Sam to answer as best you can.

1. How old is Sam?

2. What kind of courses was Sam taking?

3. What kind of work did Sam do?

4. Why did Sam move to the suburbs?

5. What kind of pet did he have?

6. How is his health?

7. What kind of exercise does he do?

8. Why does he occasionally cook with his neighbor?

9. What do you think he cooks?

10. What are his hobbies?

11. What does he enjoy doing outdoors?

12. Do you think Sam is someone you would enjoy meeting? Why or why not?

Participant D

Please think about the person who was just described to you for a moment. In the space below, write down everything you can remember about this person. When you have finished writing down what you remember, please answer the questions on the next page.

Based on your image of Sam, please answer the following questions. If you do not have enough information to answer a particular question, draw on your image of Sam to answer as best you can.

1. How old is Sam?

2. What kind of courses was Sam taking?

3. What kind of work did Sam do?

4. Why did Sam move to the suburbs?

5. What kind of pet did he have?

6. How is his health?

7. What kind of exercise does he do?

8. Why does he occasionally cook with his neighbor?

9. What do you think he cooks?

10. What are his hobbies?

11. What does he enjoy doing outdoors?

12. Do you think Sam is someone you would enjoy meeting? Why or why not?

Examine the responses of the four participants. In what ways did the shift in age or gender affect the images generated?

Thinking Further

1. Studies of the role of cognition in the stereotyping process generally indicate the following:

   - We easily and readily place others into categories.
   - We tend to pay attention to and remember information consistent with our stereotype.
   - We fill in gaps in memory with information that fits our stereotypes.
   - We tend to make judgments about causes of behavior that are stereotype consistent.
   - Discuss the extent to which the data you collected indicated any of these cognitive processes.

2. Discuss the possible sources of any stereotypes found in your data.

3. Discuss the implications of the existence of such stereotypes.

Reference

Hinton, P. R. (2016). *The perception of people: Integrating cognition and culture.* New York, NY: Routledge.

ACTIVITY 8.7
THE CONTENT OF STEREOTYPES

We know that stereotypes occur because of the human tendency to use categories to make sense of our world, but why is it that stereotypes of various groups differ from each other? For example, why is one group stereotyped as frail and helpless whereas another is stereotyped as violent and threatening? The stereotype content model developed by Susan Fiske and colleagues (Fiske, Cuddy, Glick, & Xu, 2002) can help us to understand why stereotypes vary and why they often include a combination of positive and negative attributes. These authors suggest that when we encounter someone from an outgroup, we ask ourselves two questions: (1) Does this person intend to harm me? (warmth) and (2) Is this person capable of harming me? (competence). These two dimensions, warmth and competence, determine the nature of specific stereotypes. For example, when the stereotype content model is applied to social class, people with high socioeconomic status are perceived as competent but cold, whereas people with low socioeconomic status are viewed as less competent but warmer (Durante, Tablante, & Fiske, 2017). Differences in stereotype content are important because they help to explain why a particular stereotype is associated with a specific type of treatment. This model can also guide strategies for reducing stereotyping. The purpose of this activity is to familiarize you with the stereotype content model and the implications of stereotype content for discriminatory treatment and stereotype reduction.

Directions: First identify a specific social group that you know to be stereotyped, then plot it on the dimensions below. If you are unsure as to how that group is stereotyped, you might ask for others' opinions or find research on that group.

Group _____

```
                        High Warmth
                            |
                            |
            Pity            |      Admiration
                            |
  Low       _____ | _____    High
Competence                  |                   Competence
            Disgust         |      Envy
                            |
                            |
                        Low Warmth
```

1. Based on the stereotype content model, what kind of treatment might you expect members of that group to experience?

2. Based on the stereotype content model, what might be some strategies for reducing this particular stereotype?

Thinking Further

Susan Fiske (2017) observed that stereotype content (in terms of warmth and competence) is more consistent across cultures for sex, age, and social class than for race, ethnicity, and religion. Why might this occur?

References

Durante, F., Tablante, C. B., & Fiske, S. T. (2017). Poor but warm, rich but cold (and competent): Social classes in the stereotype content model. *Journal of Social Issues, 73*(1), 138–157.

Fiske, S. T. (2017). Prejudices in cultural contexts: Shared stereotypes (gender, age) versus variable stereotypes (race, ethnicity, religion). *Perspectives on Psychological Science, 12*(5), 791–799.

Fiske, S. T., Cuddy, A. J. C., Glick, P., & Xu, J. (2002). A model of (often mixed) stereotype content: Competence and warmth respectively follow from perceived status and competition. *Journal of Personality and Social Psychology, 82*(6), 878–902.

ACTIVITY 8.8
ENEMY IMAGES

This activity seeks commonalities in the way enemies are portrayed and explores the implications of these enemy images.

Directions: For this activity you will need to locate an enemy image. This image can be either a picture or a written depiction of someone viewed as an enemy. Unfortunately, enemy images are not difficult to find. You can find enemy images in wartime propaganda, newspaper editorials, political cartoons, or in the literature of hate groups on the Internet. If possible, make a copy of the enemy image to attach to this write-up and then answer the questions below.

1. Identify the individual or entity portrayed as the enemy.

2. Describe the features of the enemy image.

3. Discuss the strategies used to associate the enemy with evil or to make the enemy contemptible to the perceiver.

4. Describe a strategy that could be used to counteract enemy images.

ACTIVITY 8.9
UNDERSTANDING ANTI-IMMIGRANT PREJUDICE

The number of refugees and other migrants across the globe has reached its highest level since World War II. The United Nations High Commission for Refugees (UNHCR, 2017) reports 68.5 million forcibly displaced people worldwide, 25.4 million of whom are refugees. Refugees are an internationally protected category of individuals fleeing armed conflict or persecution. Other people migrate to escape economic hardship, the aftermath of natural disasters, or the effects of climate change (World Bank, 2016). There are many challenges for displaced individuals seeking to resettle, including lack of resources, particularly since the majority of displaced individuals are hosted in developing nations. However, one of the biggest barriers is prejudice on the part of members of host nations. Anti-immigrant prejudice seems to be stronger among people who have greater exposure to mass media (White, Duck, & Newcombe, 2012) and may also be influenced by language. For example, the term "illegal aliens" was found to evoke greater prejudice than "undocumented workers" (Pearson, 2010). This activity will help you to become familiar with the causes of anti-immigrant prejudice and possible strategies for prejudice reduction.

One model that has been useful in predicting anti-immigrant and anti-refugee attitudes in diverse nations and contexts is Walter and Cookie Stephan's (2000) Integrated Threat Model (e.g., Esses, Hamilton, Gaucher, 2017; Ramsay & Pang, 2017). According to this model, the likelihood of prejudice increases when these components are present:

- *Realistic threats* to one's well-being, economic power, or political power
- *Symbolic threats* to one's values, beliefs, or worldview
- *Intergroup anxiety* about interacting with members of the outgroup
- *Negative stereotypes*

Directions: Citing specific news and social media sources, respond to the following questions to apply the Integrated Threat Model to anti-immigrant attitudes:

1. In your country, have immigrants been portrayed as a realistic threat? Give an example to support your answer.

---

2. In your country, have immigrants been portrayed as a symbolic threat? Give an example to support your answer.

3. Do you think nonimmigrant individuals in your country feel anxious about interacting with immigrants? Please explain.

4. In your country, have immigrants been portrayed using negative stereotypes? Give an example to support your answer.

Thinking Further

Given what you have learned about predictors of anti-immigrant prejudice, describe one action that could be taken to reduce this form of bias.

References

Esses, V. M., Hamilton, L. K., & Gaucher, D. (2017). The global refugee crisis: Empirical evidence and policy implications for improving public attitudes and facilitating refugee resettlement. *Social Issues and Policy Review*, *11*(1), 78–123.

Pearson, M. R. (2010). How "undocumented workers" and "illegal aliens" affect prejudice toward Mexican immigrants. *Social Influence*, *5*(2), 118–132.

Ramsay, J. E., & Pang, J. S. (2017). Anti-immigrant prejudice in rising East Asia: A stereotype content and integrated threat analysis. *Political Psychology*, *38*(2), 227–244.

Stephan, W. G., & Stephan, C. W. (2000). An integrated threat theory of prejudice. In S. Oskamp (Ed.), *"The Claremont Symposium on Applied Social Psychology" Reducing prejudice and discrimination* (pp. 23–45). Mahwah, NJ: Lawrence Erlbaum.

UNHCR. (2017). *Global trends: Forced displacement in 2017*. Geneva, Switzerland: Author.

White, C., Duck, J. M., & Newcombe, P. A. (2012). The impact of media reliance on the role of perceived threat in predicting tolerance of Muslim cultural practice. *Journal of Applied Social Psychology*, *42*(12), 3051–3082.

World Bank. (2016). *Forcibly displaced: Toward a development approach supporting refugees, the internally displaced, and their hosts*. Washington, DC: Author.

ACTIVITY 8.10
THE CONTACT HYPOTHESIS

Many prejudice-reduction interventions are based on the idea that if people from different groups are brought together they will learn about each other, come to see their commonalities, and prejudice will diminish. Unfortunately, studies indicate that contact does not always result in decreased prejudice and under some conditions may actually worsen intergroup relations. Gordon Allport's (1954) *contact hypothesis* outlined the specific conditions required for prejudice reduction through intergroup contact. This activity will familiarize you with the contact conditions associated with an increase and decrease in prejudice (e.g., Pettigrew & Tropp, 2006).

Contact tends to *reduce* prejudice when:

- The contact is between groups that are roughly equal in social, economic, or task-related status.
- People in authority and/or the general social climate are in favor of and promote the contact.
- The contact is intimate and informal enough to allow participants to get to know each other as individuals.
- The contact is pleasant or rewarding.
- The contact involves cooperation and interdependence.
- Superordinate goals are more important than individual goals.

Contact tends to *increase* prejudice when:

- Contact reinforces stereotypes.
- Contact produces competition between groups.
- Contact emphasizes boundaries between groups.
- Contact is unpleasant, involuntary, frustrating or tense.
- Contact is between people of unequal status.

Directions: Read the following scenario and answer the questions below based on the information provided about the contact hypothesis. This scenario illustrates the research finding that in everyday settings, there is often little intergroup contact *within* diverse populations (McKeown & Dixon, 2017).

Scenario

Although Central High School has an ethnically and economically diverse student population, there is very little interaction between groups. At lunch time, for example,

---

Asian, Black, Latino/a, and White students self-segregate into separate areas of the campus. When the principal has tried to encourage greater intergroup contact, these efforts have been met with resistance and, at times, outright hostility.

1. Discuss possible reasons for the intergroup hostility characterizing this high school setting.

2. Describe the steps you would take to reduce prejudice in the situation described.

References

Allport, G. W. (1954). *The nature of prejudice*. Cambridge, MA: Perseus Books.

McKeown, S., & Dixon, J. (2017). The "contact hypothesis": Critical reflections and future directions. *Social and Personality Psychology Compass, 11*(1).

Pettigrew, T. F., & Tropp, L. R. (2006). A meta-analytic test of intergroup contact theory. *Journal of Personality and Social Psychology, 90*, 751–783.

Intercultural Interaction

ACTIVITY 9.1
CULTURE MIXING

Although culture mixing has existed for centuries, it is a relatively new topic for cross-cultural researchers. Culture mixing refers to ". . . the coexistence of representative symbols of different cultures in the same space at the same time" (Hao, Li, Peng, Peng, & Torelli, 2016, p. 1257). There are many examples of culture mixing in food, such as the sushi burrito, ramen noodle burger, and poutine pizza. Researchers have created their own culturally mixed images, including the McDonald's Golden Arches superimposed on the Great Wall of China (Yang, Chen, Xu, Preston, & Chiu, 2016), a traditional Chinese paper-cutting in the shape of Mickey Mouse, and a Chinese porcelain plate with a picture of an American eagle in the middle (Cui, Xu, Wang, Qualls, & Hu, 2016). Several studies have focused on identifying factors that shape responses to culture mixing, since this phenomenon is expected to increase in the coming years along with globalization and more frequent intercultural contact. The purpose of this activity is to explore the nature of and responses to culture mixing.

Directions: For this activity you will first create an example of culture mixing and then gather reactions to your example from at least three people. Draw or describe your example of culture mixing in the space provided below.

Participant A

Use the rating scale below to indicate your feelings about this image:

	VERY NEGATIVE							VERY POSITIVE	
1	2	3	4	5	6	7	8	9

Please explain:

Participant B

Use the rating scale below to indicate your feelings about this image:

	VERY NEGATIVE							VERY POSITIVE	
1	2	3	4	5	6	7	8	9

Please explain:

Participant C

Use the rating scale below to indicate your feelings about this image:

	VERY NEGATIVE							VERY POSITIVE	
	1	2	3	4	5	6	7	8	9

Please explain:

1. What aspects of the image could influence reactions to culture mixing?

2. What aspects of the respondent's personality could influence reactions to culture mixing?

Thinking Further

What might be the effect of repeated exposure to culture mixing?

References

Cui, N., Xu, L., Wang, T., Qualls, W., & Hu, Y. (2016). How does framing strategy affect evaluation of culturally mixed products? The self–other asymmetry effect. *Journal of Cross-Cultural Psychology, 47*(10), 1307–1320.

Hao, J., Li, D., Peng, L., Peng, S., & Torelli, C. J. (2016). Advancing our understanding of culture mixing. *Journal of Cross-Cultural Psychology, 47*(10), 1257–1267.

Yang, D. Y.-J., Chen, X., Xu, J., Preston, J. L., & Chiu, C.-y. (2016). Cultural symbolism and spatial separation: Some ways to deactivate exclusionary responses to culture mixing. *Journal of Cross-Cultural Psychology, 47*(10), 1286–1293.

ACTIVITY 9.2
NONVERBAL COMMUNICATION

Is it possible to be in the same room as another person and not communicate? Even if we do not speak, we communicate through our facial expressions and gestures. Even if we do not move, we communicate through our posture, use of space, and appearance. Nonverbal behaviors serve several functions including complementing or accenting a verbal message, contradicting verbal cues, substituting for a verbal message, and regulating the flow of conversation (Ekman & Friesen, 1969). The ability to comprehend nonverbal communication is likely an important component of intercultural competence (Molinsky, Krabberhoft, Ambady, & Choi, 2005).

Some aspects of nonverbal behavior appear to be universal. For example, Caroline Keating and E. Gregory Keating (cited in Keating, 1994) found that in a variety of cultures tested, interpersonal distances (called *proxemics*) were closer between people who were acquainted than among strangers. In addition, the experience of crowding appears to be equally stressful across ethnic groups studied (Evans, 2000). On the other hand, there are also significant cultural differences in nonverbal behavior. Although it may be universal that acquaintances prefer smaller interpersonal distances than strangers and that people find overcrowding stressful, the preferred distance between people varies quite dramatically across cultures. According to Edward T. Hall (1966), members of low contact cultures, such as Japan, tend to prefer significantly larger interpersonal distances than U.S. Americans and Canadians, who in turn prefer larger interpersonal distances than people in high contact cultures such as many Arabs, Greeks, and Southern Italians. Individuals dealing with someone from a lower contact culture than themselves may feel rejected. Individuals dealing with someone from a higher contact culture than themselves may feel intruded upon.

Often when we think of nonverbal communication, we think of gestures that correspond to specific meanings (called *emblems*). Although the existence of emblems appears to be universal, as any traveler knows there are many cross-cultural differences in meaning. For example, the ring gesture, made by touching one's index finger to one's thumb, is used in different parts of the world with such diverse meanings as okay, a body orifice, zero or nothing, money, and Thursday (Morris, Collett, Marsh, & O'Shaughnessy, 1979). The purpose of this activity is to better understand the function of nonverbal communication and the ways it differs from verbal communication.

Directions: In the space provided below, list all of the words or meanings that you know how to express nonverbally. Then answer the questions that follow.

1. Look back to your list of nonverbal expressions. In the space provided below, write/ draw a dictionary entry for one of these expressions. It may be helpful to refer to an established dictionary for ideas about the format and content of your entry.

2. Think about the nonverbal expressions you listed above. How is nonverbal communication similar to verbal communication?

3. How is nonverbal communication different from verbal communication?

4. Do you think the potential for intercultural misunderstanding is greater in verbal or nonverbal communication? Please explain.

Thinking Further

How could you go about learning how to communicate nonverbally in an unfamiliar culture?

References

Ekman, P. & Friesen, W. (1969). The repertoire of nonverbal behavior: Categories, origins, usage, and coding. *Semiotica, 1*, 49–98.

Evans, G. W. (2000). Cross-cultural differences in tolerance for crowding: Fact or fiction? *Journal of Personality and Social Psychology, 79*, 204–210.

Hall, E. T. (1966). *The silent language*. Garden City, NY: Doubleday.

Keating, C. F. (1994). World without words: Messages from face and body. In W. J. Lonner & R. S. Malpass (Eds.), *Psychology and culture* (pp. 175–182). Boston, MA: Allyn & Bacon.

Molinsky, A. L., Krabberhoft, M. A. Ambady, N., & Choi, S. Y. (2005). Cracking the nonverbal code: Intercultural competence and gesture recognition across cultures. *Journal of Cross-Cultural Psychology, 36,* 380–395.

Morris, D., Collett, P., Marsh, P., & O'Shaughnessy, M. (1979), *Gestures.* New York, NY: Stein and Day.

ACTIVITY 9.3
CONFLICT COMMUNICATION STYLE

Much research has demonstrated cultural variability in conflict handling style. This activity will provide you with an indication of how you communicate in conflict situations.

Directions: Using the scale at the top of each page, circle the number that best describes how you feel about each of the following statements. Once you have completed the scale, calculate and plot your scores, and then answer the questions that follow.

STRONGLY DISAGREE 1	DISAGREE 2	DISAGREE SOMEWHAT 3	NEUTRAL 4	AGREE SOMEWHAT 5	AGREE 6	STRONGLY AGREE 7

1. When something I have purchased is found to be defective, I keep it anyway. 1 2 3 4 5 6 7

2. Showing your feelings in a dispute is a sign of weakness. 1 2 3 4 5 6 7

3. I would be embarrassed if neighbors heard me argue with a family member. 1 2 3 4 5 6 7

4. I rarely state my point of view unless I am asked. 1 2 3 4 5 6 7

5. I am drawn to conflict situations. 1 2 3 4 5 6 7

6. If I were upset with a friend I would discuss it with someone else rather than the friend who upset me. 1 2 3 4 5 6 7

7. An argument can be resolved more easily when people express their emotions. 1 2 3 4 5 6 7

8. I would feel uncomfortable arguing with one friend in the presence of other friends. 1 2 3 4 5 6 7

9. In a dispute, I try not to let the other person know what I am thinking. 1 2 3 4 5 6 7

STRONGLY DISAGREE	DISAGREE	DISAGREE SOMEWHAT	NEUTRAL	AGREE SOMEWHAT	AGREE	STRONGLY AGREE
1	2	3	4	5	6	7

10. I like it when other people challenge my opinions. 1 2 3 4 5 6 7

11. After a dispute with a neighbor, I would feel uncomfortable seeing him or her again even if the conflict had been resolved. 1 2 3 4 5 6 7

12. If I become angry it is because I have lost control. 1 2 3 4 5 6 7

13. I don't mind being involved in an argument in a public place. 1 2 3 4 5 6 7

14. In a dispute, I want to know all about the other person's thoughts and beliefs. 1 2 3 4 5 6 7

15. I enjoy challenging the opinions of others. 1 2 3 4 5 6 7

16. When I have a conflict with someone I try to resolve it by being extra nice to him or her. 1 2 3 4 5 6 7

17. It shows strength to express emotions openly. 1 2 3 4 5 6 7

18. I feel uncomfortable seeing others argue in public. 1 2 3 4 5 6 7

19. There are not many people with whom I feel comfortable expressing disagreement. 1 2 3 4 5 6 7

20. I don't mind when others start arguments with me. 1 2 3 4 5 6 7

21. I feel more comfortable having an argument over the phone than in person. 1 2 3 4 5 6 7

22. Getting emotional only makes conflicts worse. 1 2 3 4 5 6 7

23. I am just as comfortable having an argument in a public place as in a private place. 1 2 3 4 5 6 7

24. In a dispute, I am glad when the other person asks me about my thoughts or opinions. 1 2 3 4 5 6 7

STRONGLY DISAGREE 1	DISAGREE 2	DISAGREE SOMEWHAT 3	NEUTRAL 4	AGREE SOMEWHAT 5	AGREE 6	STRONGLY AGREE 7

25. I feel upset after an argument.   1 2 3 4 5 6 7

26. I expect a family member to know what is on my mind
    without my telling him or her.   1 2 3 4 5 6 7

27. It makes me uncomfortable when other people express
    their emotions.   1 2 3 4 5 6 7

28. I am annoyed when someone refuses to discuss a
    disagreement with me because there are others around.   1 2 3 4 5 6 7

29. In a conflict situation I feel comfortable expressing my
    thoughts no matter who the others involved are.   1 2 3 4 5 6 7

30. I hate arguments.   1 2 3 4 5 6 7

31. I prefer to express points of disagreement with others
    by writing them notes rather than speaking with them
    directly.   1 2 3 4 5 6 7

32. It is a waste of time to involve emotions in a dispute.   1 2 3 4 5 6 7

33. I argue in public.   1 2 3 4 5 6 7

34. When involved in a dispute I often become silent.   1 2 3 4 5 6 7

35. I wait to see if a dispute will resolve itself before taking
    action.   1 2 3 4 5 6 7

36. If a coworker were interfering with my performance on
    the job I would rather speak to him or her directly than
    to tell the boss.   1 2 3 4 5 6 7

37. For me, expressing emotions is an important part of
    settling disputes.   1 2 3 4 5 6 7

38. I feel uncomfortable when others argue in my presence.   1 2 3 4 5 6 7

STRONGLY DISAGREE	DISAGREE	DISAGREE SOMEWHAT	NEUTRAL	AGREE SOMEWHAT	AGREE	STRONGLY AGREE
1	2	3	4	5	6	7

39. In a dispute there are many things about myself
    that I won't discuss.   1 2 3 4 5 6 7

40. Conflicts make relationships interesting.   1 2 3 4 5 6 7

41. If a friend owed me money, I would hint about it
    before asking directly to be paid.   1 2 3 4 5 6 7

42. In a dispute, I express my emotions openly.   1 2 3 4 5 6 7

43. When I am having a dispute with someone, I
    don't pay attention to whether others are around.   1 2 3 4 5 6 7

44. In an argument I try to reveal as little as possible
    about my point of view.   1 2 3 4 5 6 7

45. Arguments don't bother me.   1 2 3 4 5 6 7

46. I prefer to solve disputes through face-to-face
    discussion.   1 2 3 4 5 6 7

47. I avoid people who express their emotions
    easily.   1 2 3 4 5 6 7

48. I wouldn't mind if a friend told others about an
    argument that we had.   1 2 3 4 5 6 7

49. During a dispute I state my opinions openly.   1 2 3 4 5 6 7

50. Arguments can be fun.   1 2 3 4 5 6 7

Scoring: This Conflict Communication Scale comprises five subscales. To calculate your subscale scores, first copy your scores from each of the items into the columns on the next page, then reverse the scoring of the items marked with an asterisk (*) so that 1 = 7, 2 = 6, 3 = 5, 4 = 4, 5 = 3, 6 = 2, and 7 = 1. Finally, sum each item in the column to calculate the subscale score.

Confrontation		Emotional Expression		Public/Private Behavior		Self-Disclosure		Conflict Approach/ Avoidance	
1*		2*		3*		4*		5	
6*		7		8*		9*		10	
11*		12*		13		14		15	
16*		17		18*		19*		20	
21*		22*		23		24		25*	
26*		27*		28		29		30*	
31*		32*		33		34*		35*	
36		37		38*		39*		40	
41*		42		43		44*		45	
46		47*		48		49		50	
Total		Total		Total		Total		Total	

Hall (1976) distinguished between low- and high-context cultures. In low-context cultures, most of what is communicated is done so explicitly. People in low-context cultures are more likely to directly state or indicate what they would like to say. In high-context cultures, the message is communicated more indirectly. For example, suppose you have asked a favor of a coworker and he is unable to offer you assistance. If this had occurred in a low-context culture, the coworker would likely tell you directly that unfortunately he is unable to help. If this same event occurred in a high-context culture, however, the coworker might indicate the same message by giving a vague reply stating that he will do his best to help.

Hall described the United States (most likely referring to the dominant culture of the United States), Germany, and Scandinavia as representative of low-context cultures and placed the cultures of China, Japan, and Korea near the high-context end of the continuum. Latin American, Greek, and Arab cultures have also been categorized as high-context. You may have observed that low-context cultures tend to be more individualistic, whereas high-context cultures are more collectivistic. According to Stella Ting-Toomey and John Oetzel (2005) high- and low-context cultures are expected to vary on several dimensions of conflict handling. In terms of the Conflict Communication Scale, we would expect low-context cultures to be characterized by greater levels of confrontation, public disputing behavior, self-disclosure, emotional expression, and conflict approach.

Average scores for each of the subscales for U.S. undergraduates are as follows: Confrontation, 48; Public/Private, 31; Emotional Expression, 49; Conflict Approach/ Avoidance, 35; and Self-Disclosure, 47. Scores below the mean indicate more indirect or high-context communication. Scores above the mean indicate more direct or low-context communication.

To what extent do your Conflict Communication Scale scores reflect low-context or high-context communication?

Thinking Further

Differences in conflict communication styles are a common cause of intercultural (and interpersonal) misunderstandings. What strategies would you recommend for resolving conflicts between individuals with opposing styles?

Source

Questionnaire items adapted from Goldstein, S. B. Construction and validation of a conflict communication scale. *Journal of Applied Social Psychology, 29,* 1803–1832. Copyright © 1999 by Wiley-Blackwell. Adapted with permission.

References

Hall, E. T. (1976). *Beyond culture*. New York, NY: Doubleday.

Ting-Toomey, S., & Oetzel, J. G. (2005). The matrix of face: An updated face-negotiation theory. In W. B. Gudykunst (Ed.), *Theorizing about intercultural communication* (pp. 71–92). Thousand Oaks, CA: Sage.

ACTIVITY 9.4
CLOCK TIME AND EVENT TIME

Robert Levine, social psychologist and author of *A Geography of Time*, suggested that one of the most profound adjustments a sojourner must make is to cultural differences in the pace of life. These differences have also been noted by individuals who move between urban and rural settings, corporate cultures, ethnic communities, and even academic disciplines. Research indicates that understanding cultural differences in time perception may be key to successful negotiations (MacDuff, 2006) and work outcomes (Nonis, Teng, & Ford, 2005). The purpose of this activity is to provide you with a better understanding of the role of temporal differences in cross-cultural adjustment.

Levine (1997; 2015) reported that a primary distinction in time perception is between *clock time* and *event time*. For cultures that follow clock time, the numbers on the clock signal when to begin and end activities. Cultures on event time, however, focus on the progression of the activity itself to determine when it begins or ends. Participants begin and end activities when it feels right to do so. Tamar Avnet and Anne-Laure Sellier (2011, p. 665) explained that "The main difference between these ways of scheduling tasks is that the decision to move to the next task is based on an internal cue in event-time versus an external cue in clock-time." From the perspective of someone on event time, for example, it would seem bizarre to end an exciting discussion or event simply because you are "out of time." Cultures using clock time tend to be far more concerned with punctuality that those on event time. For example, you may have a 7:00 p.m. appointment to study for an exam with a friend. If you are on clock time, you might arrive at 7:00 p.m., having decided in advance that you will stop studying at 9:00 p.m. since your friend has a meeting. If a neighbor drops in with a video to show you he or she might be politely informed that you are studying and can't watch it right now. However, if you are on event time, another activity may delay your arrival for the appointment with your friend. In fact, if you arrived at exactly 7:00 your friend might not be there since you are not expected to arrive at the appointed time. On event time you would stop studying when you are finished even if this means that your friend is late for the meeting. If a neighbor drops in with a video on event time, you will likely invite him or her in for a while before you resume studying. In event time, time is much more flexible and less compartmentalized than in clock time.

Directions: First determine whether the culture in which you live is best characterized by clock time or event time. Then spend one day living as best you can according to the opposite time orientation. (Most readers of this book will be accustomed to clock time and thus will spend a day using event time.) It is best to choose a day

---

when you do not have any classes, work, or life altering time commitments! Finally, respond to the questions below.

Description: In some detail, explain how you spent your day using a different time orientation and describe the emotions you experienced during this activity.

1. What priorities accompany the use of clock time? What priorities accompany the use of event time?

2. Avnet and Sellier (2011) found that even within a society, some individuals function better on clock time (people who feel that there is always room for improvement and would continue working on a task if not for the clock) and others are more effective on event time (those who persevere on a task until their internal sense tells them that there are no longer mistakes to be corrected). Which time orientation best suits you? Please explain.

3. Cultures on clock time tend to use time in a more monochronic manner. That is, activities are conducted sequentially; when one activity is completed another is begun. Cultures on event time tend to be more polychronic, conducting several tasks and social interactions simultaneously. For example, in monochromic societies people line or queue up to be served at a bank whereas in polychronic societies the teller might be helping three or four people at the same time. How might people with a monochronic orientation view polychromic behavior? How might people with a polychronic orientation view monochromic behavior?

Thinking Further

Your experience with a different time orientation may have been made more challenging because others in your environment didn't make this change. How might it be for you to travel to a culture in which you and everyone else operated on a time orientation different from your current one? What strategies could you use to adjust to such a shift in time perception?

References

Avnet, T., & Sellier, A. (2011). Clock time vs. event time: Temporal culture or self-regulation? *Journal of Experimental Social Psychology, 47*(3), 665–667.

Levine, R. (1997). *A geography of time: The temporal misadventures of a social psychologist*. New York, NY: Basic Books.

Levine, R. (2015). Keeping time. In M. Stolarski, N. Fieulaine, & W. van Beek (Eds.), *Time perspective theory, review, research and application: Essays in honor of Philip G. Zimbardo* (pp. 189–197). Switzerland: Springer.

MacDuff, I. (2006). Your pace or mine? Culture, time, and negotiation. *Negotiation Journal, 22*, 31–45.

Nonis, S. A., Teng, J. K., & Ford, C. W. (2005). A cross-cultural investigation of time management practices and job outcomes. *International Journal of Intercultural Relations, 29*, 409–428.

ACTIVITY 9.5
ACCULTURATION STRATEGIES

Much cross-cultural research has focused on acculturation. That is, the process by which people adjust to contact with a culture other than their own. John Berry (1994; 2001) has developed a model for understanding the strategies that people use in acculturation. This activity involves applying Berry's model to your own acculturation experience in order to better understand this process.

Directions: Think about an experience you have had acculturating, or adjusting, to another culture. You may have traveled outside of your country or to an unfamiliar region of your own country. Perhaps you have spent time with an ethnic group or social class different from your own. For people entering an unfamiliar academic culture, adjusting to college may even involve acculturation. In the space provided below, describe your acculturation experience (if you can't think of a time when you adjusted to an unfamiliar culture, you can ask someone you know about their acculturation experience and modify your responses accordingly). Then answer the questions based on Berry's model in order to analyze this experience.

Description of Your Acculturation Experience:

1. Berry's (1994; 2001) model includes four types of acculturation strategies: Integration, Assimilation, Separation, and Marginalization. Read the descriptions of these strategies below and think about which best describes your own acculturation strategy.

   a. *Integration* – The individual maintains his or her own cultural identity while at the same time becomes a participant in the host culture.

   b. *Assimilation* – The individual gives up his or her own cultural identity and becomes absorbed into the host culture.

   c. *Separation* – The individual maintains his or her own cultural identity and rejects involvement with the host culture.

   d. *Marginalization* – The individual does not identify with or participate in either his or her own culture or the host culture.

   Which of the four modes above best characterizes your acculturation strategy? Please explain.

2. Berry's (2001) model also includes four types of acculturation strategies adopted by the host culture: Multiculturalism, Melting Pot, Segregation, and Exclusion. Read the descriptions of these strategies below and think about which best describes the orientation of the society or group into which you acculturated.

   a. *Multiculturalism* – The society values and fosters diversity.

   b. *Melting Pot* – The society seeks assimilation.

   c. *Segregation* – The society forces separation.

   d. *Exclusion* – The society imposes marginalization.

   Which of the four modes above best characterizes the orientation adopted by the host culture in your acculturation experience? Please explain.

3. Given the acculturation orientation of the host culture, do you believe that the acculturation strategy you adopted was effective? Please explain.

Thinking Further

1. Jan Pieter van Oudenhoven and Veronica Benet-Martínez (2015) have further elaborated on Berry's integrative acculturation strategy, which they view as a form of biculturalism. These authors distinguished between those who have high Bicultural Identity Integration (Benet-Martínez & Haritatos, 2005) and thus perceive the relationship between their heritage and host cultures as harmonious and overlapping, and those who are low on Bicultural Identity Integration and perceive dissociation and tension between their two cultural identities. If you adopted an integrative acculturation strategy, do you think you had low, moderate, or high Bicultural Identity Integration? Please explain.

2. Angela-Minh Tu D. Nguyen (2013) noted that acculturation is multidimensional in that it may differ depending on the domain, such as language use, social networks, daily living habits, cultural traditions, communication style, family socialization, and cultural knowledge. Did your acculturation strategy differ depending on these or other domains?

3. What other factors may have affected your acculturation strategy? Consider, for example, your personality, your resources, the degree to which your original cultural environment differs from that of the host culture (called *cultural distance*), and the degree to which the acculturation is voluntary or forced.

4. David Sam and John Berry (2010) indicated that in general the most preferred and effective acculturation strategy is integration. In other words, those who are engaged in both their heritage culture and the culture of the host society have better well-being than those who employ other acculturation strategies. Can you think of a situation, however, in which the separation strategy might be more preferred and beneficial?

References

Benet-Martínez, V., & Haritatos, J. (2005). Bicultural identity integration (BII): Components and psychosocial antecedents. *Journal of Personality, 73*, 1015–1050.

Berry, J. W. (1994). Acculturative stress. In W. J. Lonner & R. S. Malpass (Eds.), *Psychology and culture* (pp. 211–215). Boston, MA: Allyn & Bacon.

Berry, J. W. (2001). A psychology of immigration. *Journal of Social Issues, 57*, 615–631.

Nguyen, A.-M. (2013). Acculturation. In K. Keith (Ed.), *Encyclopedia of cross-cultural psychology* (pp. 7–12). London, UK: Wiley-Blackwell.

Sam, D. L., & Berry, J. W. (2010). Acculturation: When individuals and groups of different cultural backgrounds meet. *Perspectives on Psychological Science, 5*(4), 472–481.

van Oudenhoven, J. P., & Benet-Martínez, V. (2015). In search of a cultural home: From acculturation to frame-switching and intercultural competencies. *International Journal of Intercultural Relations, 46*, 47–54.

ACTIVITY 9.6
A CULTURE SHOCK INTERVIEW

In this activity you will conduct an interview with someone who has recently had or is currently having a cross-cultural experience to explore the causes, symptoms, and stages of culture shock, or *acculturative stress*.

Directions: *Select an interviewee.* Find someone who has had or is having a signifi-cant cross-cultural experience. It should be someone who has spent at least several months in a culture different from their own. Typically, we think of culture shock as something that happens when one travels to another country. However, many other sojourns can result in life changing cross-cultural experiences. For example, when someone raised in a rural area spends time in a big city, when Students of Color attend a predominantly White institution, or when people travel to different regions of the same country they may experience culture shock.

Check for time constraints. Reserve at least 45 minutes to 1 hour for this interview. Oftentimes people are very excited about having someone to listen to their cross-cultural adventures and they may get a bit carried away with their story telling!

Alter wording if necessary. The questions are worded for the situation in which the sojourn has been completed. If you interview someone who has a sojourn in progress, you may have to alter the wording of the interview questions somewhat.

Obtain informed consent. Explain the purpose of the interview and be sure that the interviewee understands that his or her responses may be discussed in class or included in a written report.

Assure and maintain confidentiality. Be sure you tell your interviewee that you will not in any way attach his or her name to the responses in reporting or discussing the responses to the interview. It is critical that you maintain this confidentiality in order to conduct the interview in an ethical manner.

Conduct the interview. Ask the interview questions in the order in which they appear in this exercise. Be sure to take notes in the space provided or on a separate sheet. Be aware of cultural differences in interview response style. Most psychology research texts suggest that the researcher will lose "objectivity" if he or she enters into a conversation with the interviewee in order to obtain the needed information. However, in many cultures it would seem inappropriate for the interviewer not to disclose information and opinions if he or she wishes the interviewee to do so.

Provide feedback to the interviewee if appropriate. If you have some general conclusions about culture shock based on discussing or analyzing the interview data with your class you might convey these conclusions to your interviewee. Be sure to thank him or her for the time they spent assisting you with this exercise.

Interview Questions

1. What is your home culture?

2. What is your host culture?

3. What preparation did you receive for your sojourn?

4. How much time did you spend in the host culture?

5. What did you expect the host culture to be like?

6. What was your role in the host culture (for example, international student, tourist, employee, missionary)?

---

7. How did members of the host culture react to you?

8. What does the term "culture shock" mean to you?

9. Do you think that you experienced culture shock? Why or why not?

10. Please describe any phases of adjustment that you experienced. For example, did you feel differently about being in the host culture at the beginning, middle, and end of your sojourn?

11. Did you experience any negative psychological changes such as increased irritability, anxiety, suspiciousness, concern with cleanliness, or hostility toward the host culture?

12. Did you experience any positive psychological changes such as increased confidence, increased self-awareness, or greater openness to new experiences?

13. What was the hardest thing about being in the host culture?

14. What was the best thing about being in the host culture?

15. What was the funniest thing that happened during your sojourn?

16. Was there social support (from friends or relatives) available to you during your sojourn?

17. Did most of your social support come from members of your home culture, members of the host culture, or members of another culture?

18. What new skills did you develop as a result of your sojourn?

19. What was most helpful in your adjustment to the host culture?

20. Can you think of anything that would have made your cross-cultural adjustment process easier?

21. Describe your re-entry into your home culture.

22. How would you compare the difficulty of the original adjustment to the host culture with the difficulty of the readjustment to your home culture?

23. How did others in your home culture respond to you upon your return?

24. What advice would you give to a friend who is about to leave for a cross-cultural sojourn?

Though we must be very cautious when drawing conclusions based on the responses of a single individual, summarize below what you have learned about the cross-cultural adjustment process.

Thinking Further

1. Based on your interview, what recommendations do you have for designing a training session to prepare people for a cross-cultural experience? You can make your recommendations "culture-general" (skills or information that would be useful regardless of the host culture) or "culture-specific" (skills or information that fit a certain cultural context).

2. Based on the interview you conducted, develop one *testable* research hypothesis dealing with cross-cultural adjustment.

ACTIVITY 9.7
INTERCULTURAL COMPETENCE:
A SELF-ASSESSMENT

In recent decades, changes in communication, technology, transportation, immigration patterns, and policies of segregation have meant a dramatic increase in intercultural interaction. However, most of us are unprepared to deal competently with people from cultures that are unfamiliar to us. Darla Deardorff (2006, p. 249) defined intercultural competence as "the ability to communicate effectively and appropriately in intercultural situations based on one's intercultural knowledge, skills, and attitudes." Intercultural competence is particularly critical for individuals who provide essential services to others, such as teachers, medical professionals, and counselors.

A large volume of research has attempted to identify the characteristics of interculturally competent individuals. Some of these characteristics have been used to determine the type of person to *select* for intercultural or international programs or tasks. Others have been the focus of programs that *train* people to be more effective in intercultural interaction.

The components listed on the following pages were chosen because they reappear across studies of intercultural competence (such as Arasaratnam & Doerfel, 2005; Deardorff, 2006, 2011; Griffith, Wolfeld, Armon, Rios, & Liu, 2016; Leung, Ang, & Tan, 2014; Lonner & Hayes, 2004). The purpose of this activity is to provide a means for you to evaluate your own intercultural competence and develop strategies for improving areas in which you indicate a low level of competence.

Directions: Circle the number on each of the scales that follow to indicate your own level of intercultural competence. If you score 4 or below for any of the competence components, use the space provided below each item to plan strategies for increasing your level of intercultural competence. Be creative in planning strategies for improvement. These could include such actions as reading on certain topics, gaining experience in a particular circumstance, rewarding yourself for changing your behavior patterns, or practicing certain skills. Once you have completed the competence component scales and have planned strategies for improvement, please answer the questions that follow.

Traits and Attitudes

1. Respect for diverse cultures

   Strategy for improvement:

     1   2   3   4   5   6   7
     Low   High

2. Openness to new experiences

   Strategy for improvement:

     1   2   3   4   5   6   7
     Low   High

3. Tolerance for ambiguity

   Strategy for improvement:

     1   2   3   4   5   6   7
     Low   High

4. Motivation for cultural learning

   Strategy for improvement:

     1   2   3   4   5   6   7
     Low   High

5. Empathy

   Strategy for improvement:

     1   2   3   4   5   6   7
     Low   High

Knowledge

1. Cultural self-awareness

1	2	3	4	5	6	7
Low						High

   Strategy for improvement:

2. Knowledge about language differences

1	2	3	4	5	6	7
Low						High

   Strategy for improvement:

3. Knowledge about diverse cultures

1	2	3	4	5	6	7
Low						High

   Strategy for improvement:

Skills

1. Ability to manage stress

1	2	3	4	5	6	7
Low						High

Strategy for improvement:

2. Ability to build relationships

1	2	3	4	5	6	7
Low						High

Strategy for improvement:

3. Ability to generate and evaluate problem-solving strategies

1	2	3	4	5	6	7
Low						High

Strategy for improvement:

4. Communication and listening skills

1	2	3	4	5	6	7
Low						High

Strategy for improvement:

Thinking Further

Imagine that you are a manager tasked with choosing employees for an international assignment. On which of the components of intercultural competence could employees be trained? Which of the components could not be easily taught but would have to be used as selection criteria? Please explain.

References

Arasaratnam, L. A., & Doerfel, M. L. (2005). Intercultural communication competence: Identifying key components from multicultural perspectives. *International Journal of Intercultural Relations, 29*, 137–163.

Deardorff, D. K. (2006). Identification and assessment of intercultural competence as a student outcome of internationalization. *Journal of Studies in International Education, 10*(3), 241–266.

Deardorff, D. K. (2011). Assessing intercultural competence. *New Directions for Institutional Research, 149*, 65–79.

Griffith, R. L., Wolfeld, L., Armon, B. K., Rios, J., & Liu, O. L. (December, 2016). Assessing intercultural competence in higher education: Existing research and future directions. Research Report. *ETS Research Report Series*, 16–25.

Leung, K., Ang, S., & Tan, M. L. (2014). Intercultural competence. *Annual Review of Organizational Psychology and Organizational Behavior, 1*, 489–519.

Lonner, W. J., & Hayes, S. A. (2004). Understanding the cognitive and social aspects of intercultural competence. In R. J. Sternberg & E. L. Grigorenko (Eds.), *Culture and competence: Contexts of life success* (pp. 89–110), Washington, DC: American Psychological Society.

ACTIVITY 9.8
THE PSYCHOLOGY OF TOURISM

According to Colleen Ward, Stephen Bochner, and Adrian Furnham (2001), tourism is the most common form of international encounter. However, tourists may be least likely of all sojourners to have a meaningful intercultural interaction. One reason is that tourist encounters tend to superficial and are often one-way. For example, 80,000–90,000 British tourists arrive in Gambia each year for the "winter sun," yet few residents of Gambia travel to the U.K. (Jurowski & Gursoy, 2003). In this activity you will observe tourist behavior in order to explore the psychology of tourism.

Directions: Taking detailed notes, spend an hour observing the behavior of people in a location that is popular among tourists. If there is no tourist destination near you, you can observe tourist behavior on one of the many live webcams located around the world.

1. Briefly describe the tourist destination you selected.

2. Were you able to distinguish the tourists from the local people? How?

3. Describe the specific behaviors you observe on the part of the tourists.

Thinking Further

1. How might the typically brief and temporary nature of tourist-host encounters influence tourist behavior?

2. At times, tourism has been promoted as a mechanism for increasing intercultural understanding and promoting world peace (Ward, Bochner, & Furnham, 2001). Under what circumstances might tourism work toward this goal? Under what circumstances might tourism impede intercultural understanding?

3. Richard Slimbach (2010) introduced the concept of *mindful travel* to refer to the need for awareness of one's impact on the host community on several dimensions:

   - Economically – Who benefits financially from the tourists' presence (e.g., local businesses or foreign hotel and restaurant chains?)
   - Culturally – How does exposure to tourist behaviors (e.g., language or clothing) and preferences (e.g., the items they seek to purchase) shape the host culture?
   - Socially – How does the tourists' presence affect existing social structure and power dynamics (e.g., tensions between young and old, traditional and modern)?
   - Ecologically – What is the effect of the act of traveling itself (e.g., CO_2 emissions, energy use) and the behavior of travelers (e.g., water, land use) on scare resources in the host culture?
   - Spiritually – How does tourism alter the host community's sources of meaning and wisdom (e.g., religious traditions)?

Describe a strategy that could be used to promote and reward at least one of these dimensions of mindful travel.

References

Jurowski, C., & Gursoy, D. (2003). Distance effects of residents' attitudes toward tourism. *Annals of Tourism Research, 31,* 296–312.

Slimbach, R. (2010). *Becoming world wise: A guide to global learning.* Sterling, VA: Stylus.

Ward, C., Bochner, S., & Furnham, A. (2001). *The psychology of culture shock* (2nd. ed.). Philadelphia, PA: Taylor & Francis.

ACTIVITY 9.9
CROSSING CULTURES WITH CRITICAL INCIDENTS

Critical incidents are often incorporated into training to prepare people for inter-acting effectively across cultures. According to Sarah Apedaile and Lenina Schill (2008, p. 7) "Critical incidents in intercultural communication training are brief descriptions of situations in which a misunderstanding, problem, or conflict arises as a result of the cultural differences of the interacting parties, or a problem of cross-cultural adaptation and communication." With enough exposure to critical incidents and the accompanying explanations, trainees should be able to apply their knowledge to real-life intercultural situations. This activity will familiarize you with the types of critical incidents that are used to prepare people for intercul-tural interaction.

Directions: Read the example of a critical incident below then develop your own critical incident and explanation. Critical incidents can take the form of a descrip-tion, first person account, or a brief dialogue. They are designed to raise awareness about cultural differences in a variety of domains, including:

Conflict resolution	Space and time perception
Customs and traditions	Teacher–student interactions
Family relationships	Values
Formal and informal behavior	Verbal and nonverbal communication
Gender roles	Workplace expectations

Sample Critical Incident: I think I'm adjusting well to studying in Germany, but one thing that I still can't get used to is how unfriendly people are. I mean, once you get to know people they are very nice, but I can't get over the coldness of the general public. In my hometown in the U.S., I'm used to greeting people passing by on the street with a smile, but here people either ignore me, glare back, or look at me strangely. Maybe they treat me like that because they can tell that I'm a foreigner.

    Explanation: Smiling at strangers is not common in most parts of the world. In fact, in some countries individuals who smile at strangers are perceived as odd, sus-picious, or even unintelligent (Krys et al., 2016). The tendency to smile at strangers in the U.S. may stem from its immigrant history, in which smiling was a way to let others, who may not speak your language, know that you are friendly and mean them no harm.

Your critical incident:

Your explanation:

References

Apedaile, S., & Schill, L. (2008). *Critical incidents for intercultural communication: An interactive tool for developing awareness, knowledge, and skills.* Edmonton, Canada: NorQuest College.

Krys, K., Vauclair, C. M., Capaldi, C. A., Lun, V. M., Bond, M. H., Domínguez-Espinosa, A., . . . Yu, A. A. (2016). Be careful where you smile: Culture shapes judgments of intelligence and honesty of smiling individuals. *Journal of Nonverbal Behavior, 40*(2), 101–116.

ACTIVITY 9.10
A DIVERSITY TRAINING INVESTIGATION

The use of diversity training programs in organizations has grown significantly over the past few decades in response to an increasingly global and diverse workforce, a greater emphasis on working in teams, and concern about meeting legal standards (Gebert, Buengeler, & Heinitz, 2017). Such programs were developed to address sexism, racism, and other forms of discrimination while assisting members of the organization in viewing diversity as an asset (Paige & Martin, 1996). Diversity training programs vary greatly in terms of goals, content, and the method of training. Although many diversity training programs seem to be effective, others have not been able to achieve long-term change in attitudes or behavior (Bezrukova, Spell, Perry, & Jehn, 2016). The most successful programs may be those that include changes in the structure of the organization itself, such as in hiring, promotion, and leadership development (Kochan et al., 2003). This activity involves investigating the diversity training program of a single organization in order to learn more about this important form of intercultural training.

Directions: *Identify an organization* that has conducted some form of diversity training. The organization you select may be any type of business, government agency, or educational institution. In most organizations it may be best to contact the Human Resources office. In university settings, the office of student life or student affairs may also be involved in diversity training.

Make an appointment to speak with the person in charge of diversity training. It may be possible to conduct this interview over the phone, though it will likely take a minimum of 15 minutes.

Conduct the interview using the interview format included in this activity. Before conducting your interview, it will be helpful to read the "Thinking Further" response questions below as well. Be sure to thank your interviewee for his or her assistance once the interview is completed.

Answer the questions that follow in order to analyze the information that you gathered.

Name and description of organization you selected:

Interview questions:

1. Would you characterize your workforce as *diverse*? Please explain.

---

2. When did your organization start conducting diversity training?

3. What was the reason that diversity training was implemented?

4. Is the training conducted by someone from within or outside the organization?

5. Who participates in the training? Is participation voluntary or mandatory?

6. Please describe the content of the training program.

7. What do you hope will be accomplished by the diversity training?

8. Is there an evaluation or follow-up to this program?

9. Along with this training program, did your organization make any other changes to address diversity?

Thinking Further

1. Were the goals of the program *cognitive* (focused on increasing knowledge and awareness), *affective* (focused on changing the way people feel about diversity and their own ability to perform well in diverse settings), or *behavioral* (focused on teaching specific skills and changing the way people act)? Do you think it would be easier to make cognitive, affective, or behavioral changes?

2. Was the content of the program *culture-specific* (addressing the experiences of particular groups, such as women, People of Color, or sexual minorities) or *culture-general* (addressing basic ways in which groups differ, such as communication style or leadership behaviors)?

3. Was the training process more *didactic* (based on lectures or written materials) or *experiential* (based on discussion groups, role plays, or simulations)?

---

4. What criteria would you use to determine if a diversity training program has been effective?

5. In the space provided below, please give your overall assessment of the diversity training program you investigated. Do you think it will be effective? Why or why not?

References

Bezrukova, K., Spell, C. S., Perry, J. L., & Jehn, K. A. (2016). A meta-analytical integration of over 40 years of research on diversity training evaluation. *Psychological Bulletin, 142*(11), 1227–1274.

Gebert, D., Buengeler, C., & Heinitz, K. (2017). Tolerance: A neglected dimension in diversity training? *Academy of Management Learning & Education, 16*(3), 415–438.

Kochan, T. Bezrukova, K., Ely, R., Jackson, S., Joshi, A, Jehn, K., Leonard, J., Levine, D., & Thomas, D. (2003). The effects of diversity on business performance: Report of the diversity research network. *Human Resource Management, 42*, 3–21.

Paige, R. M., & Martin, J. N. (1996). Ethics in intercultural training. In D. Landis & R. S. Bhagat (Eds.), *Handbook of intercultural training* (2nd ed., pp. 35–60). Thousand Oaks, CA: Sage.

Answers

1.1
Is Psychology Culture Bound?

Although there is evidence that many psychological findings are universal, cross-cultural research has challenged each of the seven psychological concepts listed in this activity.

1. *Susceptibility to visual illusions* – A set of classic studies (Segall, Campbell, & Herskovits, 1966) demonstrated cultural differences in susceptibility to certain visual illusions. Explanations for these findings focused on differences in exposure to (a) angular structures (the "carpentered world theory"), (b) parallel lines extending into the distance (the "front-horizontal foreshortening theory"), and (c) two-dimensional representations of actual objects (the "symbolizing three dimensions in two theory").

2. *The serial position effect (primacy and recency)* – Although this effect may reflect an underlying universal tendency (even among nonhuman primates; Castro, & Larsen, 1992), culture seems to influence whether it is expressed. Studies suggest that the serial position effect may be strengthened by specific memory strategies developed through formal schooling (Wagner, 1980). In addition, narrative memory strategies such as storytelling, used in primarily nonliterate societies, may override or diminish the serial position effect. Michael Cole and Sylvia Scribner (1974), for example, found no evidence of a serial position effect in studying memory among non-schooled Kpelle children in Liberia.

3. *Social loafing* – Although research with men in individualist cultures has tended to demonstrate social loafing, studies with women across cultures and with men in collectivist cultures have had more mixed results, with some studies indicating that being in a group may actually enhance individual performance (see, for example, Karau & Williams, 1993; Klehe & Anderson, 2007; Simms & Nichols, 2014).

4. *Secure attachment* – Studies indicate a great deal of cultural variability in what is viewed as the ideal form of attachment between children and caregivers. In many cultures, stable multiple caregivers are seen as essential for raising well-adjusted children, such as among the Agta forager community in the

Philippines (Mesman, Minter, & Angnged, 2016). In other communities, for example in many Zambian households, attachment to sibling caregivers is common (Mooya, Sichimba, & Bakermans-Kranenburg, 2016). In addition, the cross-cultural validity of Ainsworth's attachment styles and the primary method used to assess them, the Strange Situation Procedure, have recently been called into question (Otto, Potinius, & Keller, 2014; Keller, 2017). These studies challenge the notion that a secure mother–child relationship as defined by Mary Ainsworth and colleagues is the key to well-being.

5. *Delusions and hallucinations* – Much research indicates that criteria for normality are culture-bound. Although World Health Organization data (Jablensky et al.,1992) indicate that visual and auditory hallucinations are found cross-culturally as symptoms of schizophrenia, these are also forms of acceptable behavior in a variety of cultures that include altered states of consciousness as part of specific rituals or healing practices (Ward, 1989). Moreover, even when delusions and hallucinations accompany mental illness, the content of these experiences may differ across cultures. For example, individuals with schizophrenia in California, United States, reported hearing disturbing, intrusive voices whereas those in Chennai, India, heard voices that provided useful guidance and individuals in Accra, Ghana, often described the voices as those of relatives and morally good (Luhrmann, Padmavati, Tharoor, & Osei, 2015).

6. *Self-serving bias* – Several studies seem to indicate that members of Western societies are more likely than members of East Asian societies to exhibit a self-serving bias (e.g., Heine & Hamamura, 2007). However, there is also considerable variation across East Asian societies (that does not seem to be sufficiently explained by levels of individualism and collectivism). For example, a meta-analysis by Amy Mezulis and colleagues (2004) found evidence of self-serving bias among Chinese and Korean participants, but not among Japanese and Pacific Islander participants. These finding may be due in part to cultural differences in motivation for and expression of self-enhancement.

7. *Pain perception* – Laboratory and clinical research indicate cultural and ethnic group differences in perception of pain. These findings have been attributed to differences in expectations and norms for pain tolerance and expression (Lu, Zeltzer, & Tsao, 2013; Rahim-Williams, Riley, Williams, & Fillingim, 2012; Stella & Schofield, 2010).

References

Castro, C. A., & Larsen, T. (1992). Primacy and recency effects in nonhuman primates. *Journal of Experimental Psychology: Animal Behavior Processes, 18*(4), 335–340.

Cole, M., & Scribner, S. (1974). *Culture and thought: A psychological introduction*. New York, NY: Wiley.

Heine, S. J., & Hamamura, T. (2007). In search of East Asian self-enhancement. *Personality and Social Psychology Review*, *11*(1), 4–27.

Jablensky, A., Sartorius, N., Ernberg, G., Anker, M., Korten, A., Cooper, J. E., Day, R., & Bertelsen, A. (1992). Schizophrenia: Manifestations, incidence, and course in different cultures. A World Health Organization ten-country study. *Psychological Medicine*, *20*, 1–97.

Karau, S. J., & Williams, K. D. (1993). Social loafing: A meta-analytic review of social integration. *Journal of Personality and Social Psychology*, *65*, 681–706.

Keller, H. (2017). Culture and development: A systematic relationship. *Perspectives on Psychological Science*, *12*(5), 833–840.

Klehe, U., & Anderson, N. (2007). The moderating influence of personality and culture on social loafing in typical versus maximum performance situations. *International Journal of Selection and Assessment*, *15*(2), 250–262.

Lu, Q., Zeltzer, L., & Tsao, J. (2013). Multiethnic differences in responses to laboratory pain stimuli among children. *Health Psychology*, *32*(8), 905–914.

Luhrmann, T.M., Padmavati, R., Tharoor, H., & Osei, A. (2015). Hearing voices in different cultures: A social kindling hypothesis. *Topics in Cognitive Science*, *7*(4), 646–63.

Mesman, J., Minter, T., & Angnged, A. (2016). Received sensitivity: Adapting Ainsworth's scale to capture sensitivity in a multiple-caregiver context. *Attachment & Human Development*, *18*(2), 101–114.

Mezulis, A. H., Abramson, L. Y., Hyde, J. S., & Hankin, B. L. (2004). Is there a universal positivity bias in attributions? A meta-analytic review of individual, developmental, and cultural differences in the self-serving attributional bias. *Psychological Bulletin*, *130*(5), 711–747.

Mooya, H., Sichimba, F., & Bakermans-Kranenburg, M. (2016). Infant–mother and infant–sibling attachment in Zambia. *Attachment & Human Development*, *18*(6), 618–635.

Otto, H., Potinius, I., & Keller, H. (2014). Cultural differences in stranger–child interactions: A comparison between German middle-class and Cameroonian Nso stranger–infant dyads. *Journal of Cross-Cultural Psychology*, *45*(2), 322–334.

Rahim-Williams, B., Riley, J. L., III, Williams, A. K. K., & Fillingim, R. B. (2012). A quantitative review of ethnic group differences in experimental pain response: Do biology, psychology, and culture matter? *Pain Medicine*, *13*(4), 522–540.

Segall, M. H., Campbell, D. T., & Herskovits, M. J. (1966). *The influence of culture on visual perception*. Indianapolis, IN: Bobbs-Merrill.

Simms, A., & Nichols, T. (2014). Social loafing: A review of the literature. *Journal of Management Policy and Practice*, *15*(1), 58–67.

Stella, S. O., & Schofield, P. (2010). Systematic review on the literature on culture and pain. *Journal of Pain Management*, *3*(4), 347–354.

Wagner, D. A. (1980). Culture and memory development. In H. Triandis & A. Heron (Eds.), *Handbook of cross-cultural psychology, Vol. 4: Developmental psychology* (pp. 187–232). Boston, MA: Allyn & Bacon.

Ward, C. (Ed.). (1989). *Altered states of consciousness and mental health: A cross-cultural perspective*. Newbury Park, CA: Sage.

Activity 1.9
Exploring the World Village

Of the 100 inhabitants:

1. *Men and Women*
   50 are men
   50 are women

2. *Age*
   25 are under age 15
   9 are over age 65

3. *Places of Origin*
   16 are Africans
   59 are Asians
   10 are Europeans

   6 are South Americans
   8 are North Americans
   1 is Oceanian (Australia, New Zealand, Papua New Guinea)

4. *Primary Language*
   4 speak Arabic
   3 speak Bengali
   5 speak English
   4 speak Hindi
   2 speak Japanese

   12 speak Mandarin
   3 speak Portuguese
   1 speaks Punjabi
   2 speak Russian
   6 speak Spanish

5. *Religion*
   2 are atheists
   7 are Buddhists
   30 are Christians
   15 are Hindus

   23 are Muslims
   12 are non-religious
   11 are other religions

6. *Education*
   14 are illiterate adults
   3 are children without access to school (about 9% of all school-aged children)
   7 hold a college degree

7. *Technology*
80 have a cell phone
42 have Internet access
18 have cars

8. Health and Well-being
87 have access to clean drinking water
30 have a reliable source of food
55 live in urban areas
22 live in substandard housing
32 lack access to toilets
1 is a refugee

25 are affected by mental health problems
15 live with a disability
1 has HIV/AIDS
15 smoke
8 are obese

9. Wealth
11 live below the internationally defined poverty line (less than U.S. $2 per day)
10 control 85% of the world's money supply

Sources

Central Intelligence Agency. (2017). *The world factbook*. Washington, DC: Central Intelligence Agency. Retrieved from www.cia.gov/library/publications/the-world-factbook/index.html

Population Reference Bureau. (2017). *2017 World population data sheet*. Washington, D.C.: Population Reference Bureau. Retrieved from www.prb.org/Publications/Datasheets/2017/2017-world-population-data-sheet.aspx

Simons, G. F., & Fennig, C. D. (2017). *Ethnologue: Languages of the world* (20th ed.). Dallas, TX: SIL International. Retrieved from www.ethnologue.com.

United Nations Educational, Scientific and Cultural Organization. (2017). *Global education monitoring report 2017/8*. New York, NY: United Nations.

World Bank. (2017). *Annual report 2017*. Retrieved from www.worldbank.org/en/about/annual-report

World Health Organization. (2017). *Disability and health fact sheet*. Retrieved from www.who.int/mediacentre/factsheets/fs352/en/

World Health Organization. (2017). World health statistics 2017: Monitoring health for the SDGs, sustainable development goals. Geneva: World Health Organization.

Activity 2.1
Functions of Cross-cultural Research

The following functions of cross-cultural research correspond to the project descriptions in Activity 2.1 (see project numbers in parentheses below), although each may fulfill additional functions as well.

1. Identifying culture-specific values, cognitive categories, or forms of behavior. (Project 5)
2. Unconfounding variables. Two variables that may be linked in one culture may be unrelated in another culture. (Project 3)
3. Expanding the range of variables. (Project 2)
4. Understanding the relationship between ecological and psychological variables. (Project 4)
5. Investigating possible human universals. (Project 7)
6. Testing the generality of psychological models or theories. (Project 1)
7. Studying the effect of cultural change. (Project 6)

Activity 3.9
Sound Symbolism

English	Mandarin	Czech	Hindi
1. beautiful (b)	mei (b)	osklivost (u)	badsurat (u)
ugly (u)	ch'ou (u)	krasa (b)	khubsurat (b)
2. blunt (b)	k'uai (s)	tupy (b)	tez (s)
sharp (s)	tun (b)	spicaty (s)	gothil (b)
3. bright (b)	liang (b)	tmavy (d)	chamakdar (b)
dark (d)	an (d)	svetly (b)	drundhala (d)
4. fast (f)	man (s)	rychly (f)	tez (f)
slow (s)	k'uai (f)	pomaly (s)	sust (s)
5. hard (h)	kang (h)	mekky (s)	sakht (h)
soft (s)	jou (s)	tvrdy (h)	narm (s)
6. light (l)	chung (h)	tezky (h)	wazani (h)
heavy (h)	ch'ing (l)	lehky (l)	halka (l)
7. warm (w)	nuan (w)	teply (w)	thanda (c)
cool (c)	liang (c)	chladny (c)	garam (w)
8. wide (w)	chai (n)	siroky (w)	chaura (w)
narrow (n)	k'uan (w)	uzky (n)	tang (n)

Activity 6.4
Culture and Mental Health Quiz

1 TRUE. Several core symptoms of schizophrenia and, to a somewhat lesser extent, depression, have been found in cultures across Africa, Asia, Europe, North America, and South America, though there are significant differences in prevalence, etiology, symptoms, treatment, and prognosis (Bhugra, 2005; Simon, Goldberg, Von Korff, & Ustun, 2002; World Health Organization, 2017).

2 TRUE. Meta-analytic research supports these findings (Jääskeläinen et al., 2013), though indicates the need for more and better designed studies on schizophrenia outcomes in developing nations. Recovery from schizophrenia in less industrialized societies may be facilitated by several factors that are more available or common than in highly industrialized societies, including support from extended family, opportunities for meaningful work, and the option to recover at one's own pace (Lin & Kleinman,1988).

3 FALSE. Across cultures studied, boys are more likely than girls to meet the criteria for Autism Spectrum Disorder (ASD). For example, a multinational comparison of Greece, Italy, Japan, Poland, and the United States found that 72% to 87% of those diagnosed with ASD in each sample were boys (Matson et al., 2017).

4 TRUE. *Karoshi*, death by overwork, and *karo-jisatsu*, suicide by overwork, are recognized forms of mental illness in Japan (Kanai, 2009). In fact, Robert Levine (1997) reported that *karoshi* hotline centers were established throughout Japan to assist workers and their families in dealing with the stress-related problems associated with working extremely long hours. In addition to the hotline, government efforts to reduce *karoshi* include clear regulations on work hours and overtime pay, public awareness campaigns dealing with mental health and power-based harassment of workers, and specialized training for counselors and medical doctors (Ministry of Health, Labour and Welfare, 2017).

5 FALSE. Pamela Keel and Kelly Klump (2003) reported documentation of anorexia nervosa in every region of the world. They suggested that bulimia nervosa, however, may be culture bound in that it requires anonymous access to large quantities of food. Research on Latina girls has identified acculturation as a risk factor for the development of eating disorders (Rodrigues, 2017).

6 FALSE. Therapists' views of "controlled drinking" treatments vary significantly across nations, with frequency of use and evidence for effectiveness increasing over the past several decades (Körkel, 2015).

7 TRUE. However, the impact of matching clients and counselors by race/ethnicity on treatment outcomes varies depending on such factors as the client's race/ethnicity, reason for seeking counseling, history of discrimination, and whether cultural issues are discussed (Cabral & Smith, 2011; Kim & Kang, 2018; Presley & Day, 2018; Swift, Callahan, Tompkins, Connor, & Dunn, 2015).

8 FALSE. Studies carried out in different cultural settings throughout the world, including North America, Western Europe, China, India, Israel, Brazil, Chile, Puerto Rico, Australia, Indonesia, Nigeria, and Thailand, have found remarkable similarity in the cluster of behaviors characteristic of ADHD (Bird, 1998; Bauermeister, Canino, Polanczyk, & Rohde, 2010). Differences do exist, however, in rate of diagnosis, which is likely due to cultural differences in the consequences for such behavior.

9 TRUE and FALSE. According to Jessica Dere and colleagues (2013), Chinese outpatients reported significantly higher levels of *typical* somatic symptoms, as compared to the Euro-Canadians, such as weight loss, decreased appetite, insomnia, psychomotor problems, and fatigue. However, Euro-Canadians reported greater levels of *atypical* somatic symptoms, such as weight gain, appetite gain, and hypersomnia, as compared to the Chinese. Furthermore, contrary to the belief that somatic symptoms are reported due to discomfort with discussing psychological symptoms, Chinese outpatients reported "depressed mood" at similar levels as the Euro-Canadians. The authors stated, ". . . it is worth noting . . . that the very concept of somatization rests on the cultural assumption that psychological symptoms are more central to depression than somatic symptoms. It is equally as legitimate to study the phenomenon of 'Western psychologization' as it is to study 'Chinese somatization'" (p. 3).

10 TRUE. Elizabeth Page-Gould (2010) summarized research showing that those who view diversity as a threat are more likely to respond to intergroup contact with stress reactions that are detrimental to physical and psychological health.

References

Bauermeister, J. J., Canino, G., Polanczyk, G., & Rohde, L. A. (2010). ADHD across cultures: Is there evidence for a bidimensional organization of symptoms? *Journal of Clinical Child and Adolescent Psychology, 39*(3), 362–372.

Bhugra, D. (2005). The global prevalence of schizophrenia. *PLoS Medicine, 2*(5).

Bird, H. R. (1998). Diagnosis and treatment of Attention Deficit Hyperactivity Disorder. *NIH Consensus Statement, 16*, 1–37.

Cabral, R. R., & Smith, T. B. (2011). Racial/ethnic matching of clients and therapists in mental health services: A meta-analytic review of preferences, perceptions, and outcomes. *Journal of Counseling Psychology, 58*(4), 537–554.

Dere, J., Sun, J., Zhao, Y., Persson, T. J., Zhu, X., Yao, S., Bagby, R. M., & Ryder, A. G. (2013). Beyond "somatization" and "psychologization": Symptom-level variation in depressed Han Chinese and Euro-Canadian outpatients. *Frontiers in Psychology*, *4*, 377.

Jääskeläinen, E., Juola, P., Hirvonen, N., McGrath, J. J., Saha, S., Isohanni, M., Veijola, J., & Miettunen, J. (2013). A systematic review and meta-analysis of recovery in schizophrenia. *Schizophrenia Bulletin*, *39*(6), 1296–1306.

Kanai, A. (2009). "Karoshi (work to death)" in Japan. *Journal of Business Ethics*, *84*, 209–216.

Keel, P. K., & Klump, K. L. (2003). Are eating disorders culture-bound syndromes? Implications for conceptualizing their etiology. *Psychological Bulletin*, *129*, 747–769.

Kim, E., & Kang, M. (2018). The effects of client-counselor racial matching on therapeutic outcome. *Asia Pacific Education Review*, *19*(1), 103–110.

Körkel, J. (2015). Controlled drinking as a treatment goal for at-risk drinking and alcohol use disorders: A systematic review. *Sucht: Zeitschrift Für Wissenschaft Und Praxis*, *61*(3), 147–174.

Levine, R. (1997). *A geography of time: The temporal misadventures of a social psychologist, or how every culture keeps time just a little bit differently*. New York, NY: Basic Books.

Lin, E., & Kleinman, A. (1988). Psychopathology and clinical course of schizophrenia: A cross-cultural perspective. *Schizophrenia Bulletin*, *14*, 555–567.

Matson, J. L., Matheis, M., Burns, C. O., Esposito, G., Venuti, P., Pisula, E., Misiak, A., Kalyva, E., Tsakiris, V., Kamio, Y., Ishitobi, M., & Goldin, R. L. (2017). Examining cross-cultural differences in autism spectrum disorder: A multinational comparison from Greece, Italy, Japan, Poland, and the United States. *European Psychiatry*, *42*, 70–76.

Ministry of Health, Labour and Welfare. (2017). White paper on measures to prevent *karoshi*. Tokyo, Japan: Ministry of Health, Labour and Welfare.

Page-Gould, E. (2010). The unhealthy racist. In J. Marsh, R. Mendoza-Denton, & J. A. Smith (Eds.), *Are we born racist?: New insights from neuroscience and positive psychology* (pp. 41–44). Boston, MA: Beacon Press

Presley, S., & Day, S. X. (2018). Counseling dropout, retention, and ethnic/language match for Asian Americans. *Psychological Services*. Advance online publication. doi: 10.1037/ser0000223

Rodrigues, M. (2017). Do Hispanic girls develop eating disorders? A critical review of the literature. *Hispanic Health Care International*, *15*(4), 189–196.

Simon G. E., Goldberg, D. P., Von Korff, M., & Ustun, T. B. (2002). Understanding cross-national differences in depression prevalence. *Psychological Medicine*, *32*(4), 585–594.

Swift, J. K., Callahan, J. L., Tompkins, K. A., Connor, D. R., & Dunn, R. (2015). A delay-discounting measure of preference for racial/ethnic matching in psychotherapy. *Psychotherapy*, *52*(3), 315–320.

World Health Organization. (2017). *Depression and other common mental disorders: Global health estimates*. Geneva, Switzerland: World Health Organization.

Activity 7.5
Aggression across Cultures: A Quiz

1 FALSE. Although there have been anthropological accounts of societies with very low levels of aggressive behavior (see, for example, Dentan's 1968 description of the Semai) "claims regarding the absence or near absence of violence in these societies turned out to be premature" (Gielen, 2004, p. 161).

2 TRUE. Douglas Fry (2017) stated that across cultures, male aggression tends to be more frequent and more damaging than female aggression. For example, greater physical and verbal aggression was observed in Japanese and Spanish males than females (Ramirez, Andreu, & Fujihara, 2001). Karin Österman and colleagues (1998) studied forms of aggressive behavior in boys and girls in Finland, Israel, Italy, and Poland. They found that in all four countries, boys were more likely to use verbal and physical aggression than girls. However, girls were more likely than boys to use indirect forms of aggression, such as excluding peers from an ingroup.

3 FALSE. According to Barbara Krahé (2016), studies using different methodologies in a wide variety of societies have found an association between exposure to media violence, such as video game use, and aggression. Craig Anderson and colleagues (2010) compared studies from Western countries with studies from Japan, China, and Singapore, and found associations between violent video game use and aggressive behavior that did not vary significantly by culture. Some researchers have suggested that the low overall levels of violence in some Asian cultures with considerable video game use, such as Japan, challenges the link between violent video games and aggressive acts. Anderson and colleagues pointed out multiple flaws in this argument, including the lack of availability of firearms in those countries as well as the context in which violence is presented. For example, although the total amount of violence on television is similar in the U.S. and Japan, the context differs such that the consequences of violent actions are portrayed much more vividly on Japanese TV, including a focus on victims' suffering. In addition, as opposed to the action and sports video games popular in Western countries, role-playing games involving text reading and cooperative fights against computer-controlled characters are more popular in Japan.

4 FALSE. The idea that aggression builds up and, if controlled or repressed, will be expressed in another form, is part of the theory of *catharsis*. Catharsis theory also predicts that levels of aggression should be reduced by engaging in – or viewing – certain "acceptable" forms of aggressive behavior, such as contact sports. Research indicates, however, that despite widespread belief

in catharsis, expressing or viewing aggression is more likely to increase than reduce aggressive behavior (Bushman, 2002).

5 TRUE. Douglas Fry (2017) pointed out that one of the most consistent findings in research on aggression across cultures is the correlation between aggression and social organization, with warfare more common in complex and hierarchical social systems as opposed to, for example, small scale bands or tribal societies.

6 FALSE. According to U.S. Department of Justice data (2015), there is actually a positive correlation between murder rate and number of executions in the United States. That is, in states with more executions, there is a high the rate of homicide, suggesting that the death penalty does not serve as a deterrent.

7 TRUE. The availability of firearms is a strong predictor of homicides in industrialized nations (Marczak, O'Rourke, Shepard, & Leach-Kemon, 2016).

8 TRUE. Nearly 2000 studies across cultures have confirmed that parental rejection is positively correlated with aggression in children (Rohner, Khaleque, & Cournoyer, 2005). For example, children's perceptions of parental rejection in families from China, Colombia, Italy, Jordan, Kenya, the Philippines, Sweden, Thailand, and the United States predicted later internalizing (e.g., fear and anxiety), and externalizing (e.g., getting into fights) behavior problems (Putnick et al., 2015).

9 FALSE. In fact, according to Richard Nisbett (1996), the reverse is true. People from the southern United States are more likely than people from the northern United States to react to affronts to their dignity with violent behavior. According to Nisbett, this region's history as a herding society has resulted in a "culture of honor" in which such violence restores the social status of the individual or family insulted. Honor cultures have been identified in parts of Mediterranean Europe, the Middle East, Latin America, and South Asia as well as the southern United States (Smith, Fischer, Vignoles, & Bond, 2013). Although alternative explanations for higher rates of homicides in honor cultures have been posed focusing on greater economic inequality in those regions (Bond & Tedeschi, 2001), a measure of culture of honor was found to be a better predictor homicide rates in a study of 49 countries than was a measure of economic inequality (Altheimer, 2013).

10 FALSE. Although many children do not report cyberbullying experiences to parents due to fear of being embarrassed, having their phone or computer confiscated, or lack of a positive outcomes, in some countries, such as China, the

majority of victims of cyberbullying report telling a parent or other adult about the incident. This finding has been explained by cultural differences in respect for adults and the authoritative power of teachers (Baek & Bullock, 2014).

References

Altheimer, I. (2013). Cultural processes and homicide across nations. *International Journal of Offender Therapy and Comparative Criminology, 57*(7), 842–863.

Anderson, C. A., Ihori, N., Bushman, B. J., Rothstein, H. R., Shibuya, A., Swing, E. L., Sakamoto, A., & Saleem, M. (2010). Violent video game effects on aggression, empathy, and prosocial behavior in Eastern and Western countries: A meta-analytic review. *Psychological Bulletin, 136*, 151–173.

Baek, J., & Bullock, L. M. (2014). Cyberbullying: A cross-cultural perspective. *Emotional and Behavioural Difficulties, 19*(2), 226–238.

Bond, M. H., & Tedeschi, J. T. (2001). Polishing the jade: A modest proposal for improving the study of social psychology across cultures. In D. Matsumoto (Ed.), *Handbook of culture and psychology* (pp. 309–324). New York, NY: Oxford University Press.

Bushman, B. J. (2002). Does venting anger feed or extinguish the flame? Catharsis, rumination, distraction, anger and aggressive responding. *Personality and Social Psychology Bulletin, 28*(6), 724–731.

Dentan, R. K. (1968). *The Semai: A nonviolent people of Malaya.* New York, NY: Holt, Rinehart & Winston.

Gielen, U. P. (2004). Peace and violence: A comparison of Buddhist Ladakh and the United States. In L. L. Adler & F. L. Denmark (Eds.), *International perspectives on violence* (pp. 161–184). Westport, CT: Praeger.

Fry, D. P. (2017). Cross-cultural differences in aggression. In P. Sturmey (Ed.), *The Wiley handbook of violence and aggression, Vol. 1.* (pp. 81–92). Hoboken, NJ: Wiley.

Krahé, B. (2016). Violent media effects on aggression: A commentary from a cross-cultural perspective. *Analyses of Social Issues and Public Policy, 16*(1), 439–442.

Marczak, L., O'Rourke, K., Shepard, D., & Leach-Kemon, K. (2016). Firearm deaths in the United States and globally, 1990–2015. *Journal of the American Medical Association, 316*(22), 2347.

Nisbett, R. E. (1996). *Culture of honor: The psychology of violence in the South.* Boulder, CO: Westview.

Österman, K., Björkquist, K., Lagerspetz, K. M. J., Kaukiainen, A., Landau, S. F., Fraczek, A., & Caprara, G. V. (1998). Cross-cultural evidence of female indirect aggression. *Aggressive Behavior, 24*, 1–8.

Putnick, D. L., Bornstein, M.H., Lansford, J.E., Malone ,P.S., Pastorell,i C., Skinner, A.T., Sorbring, E., Tapanya, S., Uribe Tirado, L.M., Zelli, A., Alampay, L.P., Al-Hassan, S.M., Bacchini, D., Bombi, A.S., Chang, L., Deater-Deckard, K., Di Giunta, L., Dodge, K.A., & Oburu, P. (2015). Perceived mother and father acceptance-rejection predict four unique aspects of child adjustment across nine countries. *Journal of Child Psychology and Psychiatry, 56*(8), 923–932.

Ramirez, J. M., Andreu, J. M., & Fujihara, T. (2001) Cultural and sex differences in aggression: A comparison between Japanese and Spanish students using two different inventories. *Aggressive Behavior, 27,* 313–322.

Rohner, R. P., Khaleque, A., & Cournoyer, D. E. (2005). Parental acceptance-rejection: Theory, methods, cross-cultural evidence, and implications. *Ethos, 33,* 299–334.

Smith, P. B., Fischer, R., Vignoles, V. L., & Bond, M. H. (2013). Understanding social psychology across cultures: Engaging with others in a changing world (2nd ed.). Thousand Oaks, CA: Sage.

U.S. Dept. of Justice. (2015). *Crime in the United States, 2014.* Washington, DC: U.S. Dept. of Justice.

Appendix

Resources on Culture and Psychology

Internet Resources

Online Readings in Culture and Psychology

A collection of essays on a wide variety of topics in cross-cultural psychology.
https://scholarworks.gvsu.edu/orpc/

Pew Research Center's Global Attitudes Project

Public opinion surveys from around the world on a broad array of subjects including intergroup relations and perceptions.
www.pewglobal.org/

Society for the Teaching of Psychology Presidential Taskforce on Diversity Education

Annotated bibliographies of diversity teaching resources, including books, book chapters, journal articles, films, websites, and other media.
http://teachpsych.org/diversity/ptde/index.php

Understanding Prejudice

Extensive collection of information and resources on prejudice and prejudice reduction.
www.understandingprejudice.org/

World Health Organization

Publications and fact sheets on a wide variety of international health issues.
www.who.int/

World Values Survey

Data from surveys of values and beliefs in nearly 100 countries.
www.worldvaluessurvey.org/wvs.jsp

Graduate Programs in Culture and Psychology

Graduate Programs in Cross-Cultural Psychology and Education

www.iaccp.org/postgraduate

Journals

Arab Journal of Psychiatry
American Indian, and Alaska Native Mental Health Research
Asian American Journal of Psychology
Asian Journal of Social Psychology
Cross-Cultural Management
Cross-Cultural Research
Cultural Diversity and Ethnic Minority Psychology
Cultural Diversity and Mental Health
Culture, Health, and Sexuality
Culture, Medicine, and Psychiatry
Culture & Psychology
Disability and Society
Ethnic and Racial Studies
Ethnicity and Health
Ethos
Frontiers: The Interdisciplinary Journal of Study Abroad
Hispanic Journal of Behavioral Sciences
Interamerican Journal of Psychology
Intercultural Education
International Journal for the Psychology of Religion
International Journal of Cross-Cultural Management
International Journal of Culture and Mental Health
International Journal of Intercultural Relations
International Journal of Psychology
International Perspectives in Psychology: Research, Practice, Consultation
Journal of Asian Pacific Communication
Journal of Black Psychology
Journal of Black Studies
Journal of Cognition and Culture
Journal of Cross-Cultural Gerontology
Journal of Cross-Cultural Psychology
Journal of Ethnic and Cultural Diversity in Social Work
Journal of Homosexuality
Journal of Latina/o Psychology
Journal of LGBT Youth
Journal of Multicultural Counseling and Development

Psychology and Developing Societies
Psychology of Women Quarterly
Race and Social Problems
Sex Roles
Social Identities: Journal for the Study of Race, Nation, and Culture
Transcultural Psychiatry

Professional Associations

American Anthropological Association

www.americananthro.org

American Psychological Association

www.apa.org

> Division 9 – The Society for the Psychological Study of Social Issues, www.spssi.org
>
> Division 35 – Society for the Psychology of Women, www.apadivisions.org/division-35
>
> Division 44 – Society for the Psychological Study of Lesbian, Gay, and Bisexual Issues, www.apadivisions.org/division-44
>
> Division 45 – Society for the Psychological Study of Culture, Ethnicity and Race, http://division45.org/
>
> Division 52 – Division of International Psychology, https://div52.org/
>
> Taskforce on Indigenous Psychology, www.indigenouspsych.org/

American Psychological Society

www.psychologicalscience.org

Asian American Psychological Association

www.aapaonline.org

Asian Association of Social Psychology

www.asiansocialpsych.org

Association of Black Psychologists

www.abpsi.org

Australian Psychological Society

www.psychology.org.au

British Psychological Society

www.bps.org.uk

Canadian Psychological Society

www.cpa.ca

International Academy for Intercultural Research

www.intercultural-academy.net/

International Association of Applied Psychology (IAAP)

www.iaapsy.org

International Association of Cross-Cultural Psychology (IACCP)

www.iaccp.org

National Latina/o Psychological Association

www.nlpa.ws

Psychologists for Social Responsibility

Resources for the promotion of peace, social justice, human rights, and sustainability. www.psysr.org/

Society for Cross-Cultural Research (SCCR)

www.sccr.org

Society for Disability Studies

http://disstudies.org/

Society of Indian Psychologists

www.aiansip.org/

Social Justice Organizations

Anti-Defamation League

www.adl.org/

Simon Wiesenthal Center

www.wiesenthal.com

Southern Poverty Law Center

www.splcenter.org
www.tolerance.org

Made in the USA
Monee, IL
22 February 2021